THE COLLECTED WORKS OF
KATHLEEN TANKERSLEY YOUNG

KATHLEEN TANKERSLEY YOUNG

The Collected Works

Edited by Erik La Prade & Joshua Rothes

EMPYREAN SERIES No. 20

---

about   Books reproduced herein: *Ten Poems*, Parnassus
            Press (1930); *The Dark Land*, The Dragon Press
            (1932); *The Pepper Trees*, Modern Editions Press
            (1932).

copyright The published works of Kathleen Tankersley
            Young contained in this volume [on pages 3–171]
            are in the public domain. The preface, notes, and
            biographical timeline are © 2022 Sublunary Edi-
            tions. The edited compilation of Young's unpub-
            lished works [on pages 173–210] is © 2022, Erik
            La Prade and Joshua Rothes.

isbn   978-1-955190-27-5

lccn   2022938255

CONTENTS

179   Selected Unpublished Works

PREFACE

Kathleen Tankersley Young is one of the great ghosts of modernist letters, a poet and editor thoroughly engrossed in the most exciting stylistic currents of the time, influential in shaping publications and poets alike, and yet almost entirely forgotten after her tragic death in 1933.

From the paltry fragments of biography left to us through dry historical records and rich but evasive correspondence, we can draw only a tentative portrait of her, and it seems likely she would have preferred it that way. As she was assisting the poet Charles Henri Ford with his new publishing venture, *Blues: A Magazine of New Rhythms*, in 1928, she cautioned: "No information about me in the magazine please especially about age."[1]

Kathleen Tankersley was born in rural West Texas, likely in Sonora, on August 15, 1902, though she subsequently gave her place of birth as Cincinnati (but on April 15th of 1903) and New York (in 1905, no less), depending on the circumstance. She attended high school in San Angelo, Texas, but there is no record of her having graduated, nor are there any records to back up the claims that she attended the University of Texas at Austin, Columbia, or Harvard, which appeared in various newspaper profiles over the years, most after her death.

She married twice. The first marriage took place on February 1, 1921, just hours after the death of her mother, whose dying wish—according to a widely syndicated newspaper item at the time—was for the wedding to go forward as planned. Her

1. In a letter in the Beneicke Digital Archives dated December 21, 1928, accessed at: https://collections.library.yale.edu/catalog/17425185

husband, Henry Coulter Young, was, in fact, a student at the University of Texas at Austin, where he was a member of the famed Longhorn band, a clarinetist. Their marriage was not a long one, however, as Henry would die of tuberculosis in 1925. Meanwhile, Kathleen's father had died in a wagon accident in 1924. This period of sudden loss undoubtedly colored her work.

While she was a member of the Poetry Society of Texas from 1923–1925, her first published poem did not appear until 1926, a scant five lines in *The Houston Post-Dispatch*[2]. The most fruitful period of her publishing career was the five-year span of 1927–1932, from which nearly all of the pieces included here are taken. This period also saw her establish herself as an important editorial force, first joining the staff of Denver-based magazine *The Echo*, before helping the poet Charles Henri Ford—whom she met in February 1928 at an exhibition at the San Antonio library, connected by mutual friends Lew Ney (Luther Widen) and Ruth Widen (née Wilson)[3]—bring to life *Blues: A Magazine of New Rhythms*, billed as an American answer to *Transition*, the avant-garde magazine published by Eugene Jolas out of Paris. In 1932, she would become co-editor with Eric Naul—a figure of shadowy and uncertain existence in his own right[4]—of the Modern Editions Press, publishing an influential batch of poetry pamphlets that included work by Paul Bowles, Carl Rakosi, Laurence Vail, Horace Gregory, Kay Boyle, and others, as well as

---

2. See pp. 79

3. Lew and Ruth would be instrumental in Kathleen's early publishing career, allowing her space in their magazine *Parnassus*, as well as printing her first book, *Ten Poems* via Parnassus Press in 1930. They would publish a selection of Kathleen's letters after her death in *The Latin Quarter-ly*.

4. The few letters bearing the signature of Eric Naul can be found in the Horace Gregory papers, dated after Kathleen's death. It was almost certainly a pseudonym.

two pamphlets of her own work.

As lofty as her poetic ambitions appeared to be at times, she published essentially wherever she could, from magazines of both international stature like *Transition* and Harriet Monroe's *Poetry* to those of scarcely regional note. When Ford called into question why she sent poems to the little magazines of Ben Musser, she replied, "By god I sing for the joy of singing . . . and let it be printed where it will."[5]

Her second marriage, to an Air Force lieutenant named David James Ellinger in July of 1929, was fraught from the beginning, with Young telling Ford before the wedding even took place that she made clear that she would require at least half the year to herself. In the August immediately following the wedding, she would write to Ford of her intention to move into a downtown studio by herself.

Kathleen was never one to be pinned down, and she alluded to numerous affairs in letters, with women and men, including one with *Alhambra* editor Angel Flores, who would publish her second book of poetry, *The Dark Land*, through his The Dragon Press, and whose notes are seen in the margins of her typescripts thereof.

Young also revealed in various letters that she suffered from several chronic ailments, none of which she names directly, but we can surmise that they included lung disease and a condition of the nerves. In the spring of 1928, she suffered a stomach hemorrhage for which she had an operation later that summer, possibly brought on by heavy drinking, a vice she admitted to regularly in letters. Following the operation, she was given morphine to manage residual pain; while we cannot be certain this was her first experience with the opiate, it would be a substance that would

5. Her reply, by her own account, taken from a letter to Lew and Ruth dated May 20, 1929, via Princeton University Library, .

haunt her the rest of her life.[6] Her seeming foreknowledge of her death, as well as cryptic references to barrenness and sterility, would also shade her poetry.

In 1933, she went on a trip to Mexico, alone, by some accounts suffering the deep depression of an artist unable to produce new work, afraid, as some of her acquaintances relayed after her death, that "she was losing her mental capacity", telling them that "she wished to die in order to free her soul."[7] Her state deteriorated quickly. The local vice consul was summoned to her room on multiple occasions, where he found her "in such a state of coma from morphine, other opiates and alcoholic drinks, that she was unable to talk".[8] She was found dead on April 9, 1933, of apparent Lysol poisoning. It was ruled a suicide, though doubts remain.

Kathleen Tankersley Young was a figure at once stubbornly peripheral and certain of her own unique place in the firmament of letters. Her poems and short stories drew numerous comparisons— to E.E. Cummings, James Joyce, Eugene Jolas, among others—all of which she flatly denied. If Ford is credited with having introduced surrealist motifs into American poetry, Kathleen's work, in places, begs reappraisal. What her works unequivocally do is to give voice to the experience of a *sui generis* figure in American literature, a woman from nowhere, in the thick of it all.

6. In an undated letter to Charles Henri Ford in the Beneicke Digital Archives at Yale Library, likely late 1929, early 1930, Kathleen writes of an apparent morphine overdose.

7. "Lay Poetess' Death to Fear", *San Antonio Light*, April 13, 1933.

8. Report issued by Vice Consul J. Frank Points, American Consulate, Torreón, Mexico, April 10, 1933.

NOTE ON THE TEXT

We have opted to present Young's work by leading off with the
three books she published in her lifetime, *Ten Poems*, *The Dark
Land*, and *The Pepper Trees*. (*Apology for Love*, which appeared in
1932 as a standalone pamphlet through the Modern Editions Press,
was also included in *The Dark Land*.)

In the section of her uncollected works, we opted for a chron-
ological presentation, which is likely imperfect due to trouble in
dating some poems. This section concludes with "House Full of
Windows", which appeared only posthumously, alongside her
obituary in the *San Antonio Light*.

While it is difficult to say for certain how close we have come
to a volume that might suggest the word *complete*, we can say with
great certainty that the first two sections of this book represent the
vast majority of Young's published works. She has made it difficult
on us; in her papers, she compiled a list of all of her publications and
acceptances, which included several pieces that were never published.

And finally, we present a selection of nearly forty unpublished
works, drawn primarily from two manuscripts, *Two Preludes to a
Marginal Darkness* and *City Without Images*—which were prepared
but never published, with about half the works being subsumed
into *Ten Poems* and *The Dark Land*. Where a poem appeared in both
Preludes and *City Without Images*, we have opted to publish the
version from the latter, which was a much more polished manuscript prepared after *Preludes* was assembled.

For intrepid souls who may wish to further the work done
here, there is still the task of compiling and dating her letters, as
well as attributing the unsigned (and possibly pseudonymous)
works she published in an editorial capacity for *The Echo* and *Blues*.
And doubtless somewhere, in some attic, there sits a trunk.

The Collected Works

TEN POEMS
(1930)

1.

These are mad days:
I, walking the same streets
Biting on bitter twigs, on leaves,
Feeling but little: at times I forget
How it was that I lost you,
And forget to think how it was I might have kept you,
At times it is just wind and dust
In the narrow streets where we had walked.
The endings of these days are the same:
The quick descending evening
Taking on darkness, and peering women,
The street lamps moving together as if dancing,
The houses opposite with squares of people, laughing:
What do you think at evening? Do you think
Of moons swinging over black waters, or the bays
Rocking the great boats against the stars?
Do you think of music, of leaving,
Of departing from music at midnight?
Do you sit at supper tables with dark women
Talking about nothing? What do you do?
These days are the same:
Tomorrow, a morning, and it is swallowed:
I walk along the same streets and hear the wind,
Sometimes the wind carries the thick boat whistles,
Sometimes voices, sometimes it is empty:
I go, biting on bitter twigs, on leaves,
Feeling but little:
Tomorrow, a noon, it is dried

And blows away like fine dust:
An afternoon will follow: the usual hot sleep:
And tomorrow again an evening, and the women in the streets,
And children in doorways, and people at supper tables:
Will this never end?
I would rather a great blue bullet were fired,
Exploded in every house and street in all the world,
And all the people lay dead,
And you, in your country,
With tulips in your courtyard, and wine on your table,
And the wind taking no note of you:
This would be preferable to bitterness:
Think: the wind in many houses, and every person lying still
Having the same sleep,
The same flowers blooming, the same wind.

2.

Orchids   orchids   are as nothing
Now that you are walking through the snowfall winds
Walking through the blue froststreets
Dreaming of fires, dreaming of sleep:
Orchids   orchids   are as nothing
When you never come:
But the streams keep flowing, and the rain,
Over the jungle trees tangled with heavy moon:
Orchids are as nothing,
And the wind from northern countries, tempered by water,
Tempered by tropic land,
Is not your wind, this wind tearing the orchids,
Tangling their heads:
My sleep is not a thick sleep,
But a waking, and a knowing,
A confusion of sleep, orchids, I: all nothing
Dead in the thick shell of oblivion.

3.

Here in this brittle city we contend
With stone and star and voice,
Knowing that there is no returning
And that forever we shall wander
And the edges of self recede
Until the swift and errorless sleep begin:
Flowers we have pulled in childhood,
Grass we have slept upon, stones we have gathered
To fling away again, the prayers said
By a thin candlelight, running in the wind,
Skating on the bright pavements
Where the pigeons fell, the swans we fed at nine,
The ring is gone, I threw it in,
Sunshine and snow above us, about us, and myself
In the huge sandstorms set between mountains,
The continent before us, the world is yours to conquer,
Threads pulled from bright sweaters, snow birds
Taking the crumbs from the blue fingers,
Mother in the evening weeping,
Rafts that carried us away, faster they go beyond the continents
How fortunate it is to go, the midnight in the autumn rain
When I waking could only sob and not be still again,
Mexicans singing under the window in their violent voice,
The wind over the mountains, when the whistle blows
That is the sign to gather in the schoolhouse
One whistle means fire, the other, rebels,
And we watch all day on the mountain line, we see figures
Moving, for me they are very strong, and they are there,

Mother says they are not,
At night in terror I see them surrounding us:
Leaves that were swept before us as we ran
The long terraces and the ponds
And flowers that flew to brilliant pieces in the wind,
On these terraces were peace,
I dreamed to float over these forever and never awaken:
The boats on the pond are made of paper,
They whirl with the gusts of wind, and soon they are tilted,
Soon we cannot reach them and they are carried slowly down:
Leaves, too, are boats,
We have launched them but cannot take them, we see
Them carried, and mark the quivering waters with our small
    white hands:
The balls were white and red: sometimes, o, often, we fell:
We lost consciousness in these falls, and they were full of terror,
We were glad to be back again:
O terror mounting through these days,
The world beholds us as we walk
With the stiff bodies and the barren minds,
Talking these days into disenchantment,
Lying these nights without perfect sleeping,
Crying in our sleep, and putting our hands forward
To touch a frozen wall.

4.

The dark now resembles your head
Which is (without doubt) a huge black gourd
Containing a great deal of casual bitterness:
We put out our hands and the winds walk with us:
The wet irises grow thick and white under the spring windows:
The broken hedges are slow with rain:
o the night flowers darkly and suddenly
Your thin hand trembling under the great green stone
Shakes off the last vestige of dream where a light might fall:
And thus s l o w l y the beautiful inconsequence will begin.

5.

By this recurrence we come up from days
Ending in blue butterflies
And the armrings dangling
The cocks crowing after the hens
The mint in your yard among your flowers
The bullfights in the hot towns
The mad Spanish language hurled down the goat-wandering streets
The rainy season weighting the palms
Changing we perform these duties
Open the helium atom and pry out its contents
A maniac? Surely.
To a hotel which had a Christmas tree with yellow lights
This responsibility continues
Two hundred of these copies
Seventeen albatrosses veered and wheeled
What became of the list mailed Friday
Motor boat service in season
We descending into the lake
Wearing white clothes
Gave ourselves up to the current that swept us beyond the
    cypress trees
Everyone is surprised with the result
The cooling process has begun
We came down from the maddened days
Into rain that stood upon the stone shaded streets
Into the pigeons whirling among blues of night
Into the canyons of stone: into this city
The voices were black on the side-streets

They sang a little under the brighter lights
We moved and read the hands of clocks
And believed in this city
My way of turning my back upon life to die
With your body and this sleep
Between the outer and the inner
The nightmare of subways, the thunder of trains
The people people staring staring
The blank sunshine upon entering the street
Toward you toward you and upon this plane
Do I know if these houses would stand up
If I were not in their same movement
Bat, the bad boy, the beach, the white collars
This is my body which has not been purified
From these days we went down to sleep
And the summer was hot upon us
The laughter from the far beaches
And the children swinging under the trees
And names written upon vacant houses
And cars rattling softly in the streets
We descended to sleep through this bright weather
A little softer these colors, are these buildings,
Are these streets, a little dimmer are the voices,
A little stranger are these figures
Changing we shall see the sea again
From these swift descending days
We shall see the snow again brushing the water
And hear the cold gulls screaming
And labor through the long night upon seas
Going to strange lands
Turning I am confronted by endlessness
We run away and are defeated

Give me some signal: all the signs are gone:
All the signs are gone, Beloved
I stand upon this edge of sleep
When I die I shall not have died
Because I have not existed
In your mind perhaps, within the minds of others,
I have moved and been consumed by movement

I leave you this summer sadness
Of seaplanes droning above cities
And pale beaches running with laughter
And hurdy-gurdy men stumbling along the street ways
And people leaning upon the dusty park benches
At least I have preferred the black days and the hard winds
And people hurrying into houses
And stone streets frozen over
And dead birds falling into the iced rivers
And swans and their kind seeking strange refuge
And the sleep of certain reptiles and certain animals
In their decayed tree-trunks, in their earth-holes, in their lairs
I prefer the heavy streets and the blue breath of horses
And old men dying by the hearth-fires
And blackness that enters the minds of children
And the illnesses and the fevers
Not this brightness
Not this laughter, not these meaningful sounds lurking everywhere
About us, but the slow black arcs of sleeping and no flowers
And nights full of wind and hunger
And the fogs blotting out the worn faces
I prefer to leave you this summer
And your streets through the cities
And your adventures, and your experiences,

But these will not continue beyond you:
Think: you will die in my mind when
I have left you: and that when you
Are no longer in these bright streets
You will die in others who no longer see you
By this recurrence we have come upon
Days descending into sleep
He tossed hat, coat, waistcoat
A knife, a stream of pebbles
Over the cliff with gleeful zest
Before deciding it was time to jump.

6.

Will we ever hold the shells again,
Or walk over the reddened sand?
The waters break, and we are broken,
We cry all night in our sleep:
The ships have diverged and gone the strangest directions:
The night brings further water, and the seaweed wreathes
In quick succession, and the sound is higher,
It mounts into our dreams.
Who lives beneath this sea?
The weather changes at dawn, a heavy wind comes without birds:
Slowly we begin to think of death. Our amber eyes will drift
Lightless over the sea depth:
Will the waters part again?
Will we ever know our land?

7. PREFACE TO A LETTER

Beloved, when the mornings ripen
And the pianos begin
In obscure houses on the shaded streets
To give forth mundane notes,
And the hands of children
Fall to the keys, where the windows send their soundings outward,
And the whole of steady tree shadow
Slides at once along the length of street,
A doubt grows in my mind, as I remember
In the childhood of myself, a figure
In blue linen, carrying roses
To schoolrooms to the woman
Whose hair flamed crimson, as: *this*
Is the principle, and the example
Will follow:
               Later I am consumed
With piano practice in the evening,
Lighting a candle above me on the piano,
Thinking of the Virgin Mary,
While mother weeps (I do not understand)
For the notes dropping
From my thin hands that shall be taught
To wear bright rings,
To carry roses to flaming women:
She weeps softly, and the notes go on dropping,
I, saying, *Ave Maria, Hail Mary, Blessed are thou,*
To the end.

Beloved, when the mornings
Ripen under trees trembling in their shadow,
And pianos shed their pallid untimed notes,
Doubts grow in my mind:
                              I doubt that we have listened
To chimes of clocks in the steeple
Of black churches, to glass breaking, dropped
By unseen fingers in the dark.
I doubt that we have been at all.
I doubt that we have seen the afternoon
Turned evening by early rain upon the avenue,
Or that we have walked under the long structure of the El trains
Crossing a wet street in October,
I doubt that we have been.

There are no prints that remain on the stair-rails
Where my hands have been,
Nor on the moving doors of trains of undercities,
Nor on the polished rails of omnibuses, when the light globes
In the park hung downward like gold fruit:
Leaves I have pulled to stand in vases on black mantles
Have not remembered,
Nor half burned candles lighted by a match
Held between the first and second fingers of my hand,
Nor roses broken from tall bushes to be given to flaming women,
There are no prints on the old scarred hedges
To show that my hands and breasts and limbs passed through,
Singing. They do not remember.
I doubt that I have been at all.

Beloved, when the mornings ripen
And the pianos begin

Upon the April streets, tossing their brittle notes
From the dusty window ledges,
There are things I half remember:
Other selves, and obscure figures
Carrying my shrill name to doorways,
As if this dream had no beginning,
And no ending.
The mood of the morning and the pianos, gives the question,
And I am unanswered.
When I walk homeward to a greying house
On the street of pianos,
I will write your name upon a paper,
Asking
       Have I (have we) been at all?
And in what mirror,
In what voice,
In what knowledge,
In what figure,
In what name
That has been called?

8.

Once we were warriors in this ancient city,
But now our swords are broken
And our armour rusted, yet we are held,
And gladly, too: there's nothing to go back to
That we remember:
The battlements are now defeated, and we stand
Seeing the yellow crocus in the yards, the streets
Blown down with spring, and turn, and have not any weeping:
Sudden sunlight is shot into our window:
What shall we do?
There's nothing to arise for:
Our books lie open on the floor:
One bird sings in a terrible monotone.
They say our land has been defeated utterly,
That all the dooryards that we knew have crumbled,
And the trees standing, bleed brokenness:
This may be true: our hill changed, where May stood
        deep in flowers,
The singing multitude of waters quiet,
But these are not changed more
Than you are, sitting in the sudden sun,
Than I.

9.

O the purity of blue.
We were swimming in the lakes, Mother
When the sun was eaten by the big bear mountains
Leaving only the blue air.
But why should I give up now,
There's Paris in the Spring, Mother,
We'll go to Paris
And think about hyacinth buds, or the mountains.
Without the between what would we be?
We read long into the night
By blue lights. O the purity of blue.
Le temps est venu,
But nothing else is ready,
Only the hyacinths and their buds:
We'll strike the stalk here, and the bulb.
Remember our love no matter what happens,
Water on the colored reefs, bathers in the wind, anything.
This we must keep,
And the thought of how it rained in November
And the streets stood muffled with the sound
Until the last voice was drowned.
No matter anything
But that we were.
But that was not what happened,
Instead, the days began to fall
Like leaves from an autumn tree,
And soon we were bereft.
Still I have sat here and

Of course I have remembered too much,
Having so little to do,
Everyone knows that is the trouble.
The clatter of horses' hoofs came up to my window at Christmas,
From a foreign street,
I heard the children screaming,
And turning a little I saw their fireworks
Spatter blood on the sky.
Le temps est venu,
And a thousand machines plowed through my mind
Without recovering you.
The mornings began at six
With crisp cool sheets, and red cut roses,
It wasn't so windy at morning,
But the wind came out of noon
And rocked the palm trees:
Rain came in the afternoon at three,
And then the wind again.
The old man died who cried in his sleep:
Better off,
And the wheels whirred him beyond the hall.
Not dreaming we left the market.
I'll never be so happy again.
That's the island where they keep the lepers.
The market stall of herbs was so sweet.
What did the rotting lepers think?
Mood is no continuity.
We went down the street
And the trees swallowed us,
We came out later on the foredeck laughing.
We were tired.
That was the beginning.

Islands there are so blue, Mother,
It is the coral that holds the changing colors,
Not the color of mountain lakes, Mother.
We were not allowed to swim.
We have known the wind to change.
The Spring is a bitter different thing.

10. SOUTHERN VOYAGE

Here where the white ship cuts the waves
And the thick colored mists grow bluer than on any other sea,
Gulls have trailed their circled shadows
Like a hand dipped in water, and drawn out:
Here the buoys moan,
And the heavy rivers are lost forever to the land,
And all the great gold sequences of
Moon and sun go over:
Here where the ship horns dull the distant air,
And the engines throb too loudly,
Evenings fall in a clearer way,
And gulls have a manifold reality, like hands
Dipped in water and withdrawn:
Under this water that rocks
Eternal color of blue,
Old shells are stirred,
And the dark land, diverse
With filtered greens, trembles, and is still.
There is some other element here,
Some fiercer blackness under water,
Although the light grows deep
And thick with sun:
Here the last dark land is quiet:
Here on this ancient water
There is but little remembrance:
It is as if we had never talked:
Here now the winds walk on the water,
And nothing is still but the black lost land
Lying deeply, darkly, under.

THE DARK LAND

(1932)

"Open your eyes now. I will. One moment. Has all vanished since? If I open and am forever in the black adiaphane. *Basta!* I will see if I can see.

See now. There all the time without you: and ever shall be, world without end.

. . . .

Come. I thirst. Clouding over. No black clouds anywhere, are there? Thunderstorm. Allbright he falls, proud lightning of the intellect, *Lucifer, dico, qui nescit occasum.* No. My cockle hat and staff and his my sandal shoon. Where? To evening lands. Evening will find itself."

James Joyce, *Ulysses*

APOLOGY FOR LOVE

Your head was laid on this pillow
Without the body,
And I saw the knife-cut
Where this head had been slit from the shoulders
And yet did not bleed:
I did not dream that
But through the summer and hot evening streets
The green deer ran seeking an outlet
Back to the forest,
And was plunged into waters
That surrounded the island:
Elephants colour of evening
Plodded through the streets
Chained one by one so that none of them
Was free from the others,
And they went into the park
To give their summer performance
Among children:
And then again by the sea
The beaches were trampled down
By sea-horses colour of sunset
And they walked over us but left no marks
Although the sand was badly damaged:
The candles were blue
And their flames grew larger
And we sat at the black table
And soon they were torches
And soon the room was in ashes

But there was no smoke
And we were not destroyed:
I was beginning to sleep
When a rap sounded on my door,
And when I answered
A girl with red eyes came in saying:
The music is over
And the voice kept saying:
The music the music is over.

THE CATS WALK UP AND DOWN AND CRY

The cats walk up and down
And cry, and the snow begins to fall, down, down,
Over the red trees, and women
Go through the park with their heads covered and their knees:

At twelve o'clock we wrap the red shawl round,
And wait for the miracle, and our hands freeze to these
Pencils, and these books fade red upon the palm,
And the candles set the curtains to a blaze:

The streets are filled with people who go quickly,
Faster, faster, and the snow begins slowly:
It unwinds over the boats and their whistles,
And over our house now in flames, and over

The cats walking up and crying,
And over all the late dray horses whose breath
Is blue on all the streets,
And who call one to the other.

WE ARE NOT WALKING ON LEVEL GROUND

We are not walking on level ground,
A street-organ nearby is fast grinding music,
And the organ-man's parrot blinks in the green light:
Wind blows upward through the evening
Where the green lamps spread like pools
In which we dip our feet and then emerge:
Later the light is red and others walk through blood
But have no stains that stay with them:
Late kites are caught and whirled beyond
The tiny hands that launched them,
They will be eaten by the blue black clouds,
They will touch the land of thunder:
Goodbye   goodbye
The orange-man is at the curb
Touching the scarlet fruits and crying his call:
A man sells grapes, yellow
As the evening, sweet from the watered vineyards:
Children skate and whirl past corners
Crying the names of others far ahead:
Goodbye   goodbye
Evenings they drag the black dolls home,
Thunder is in the sky, and the sound of voices in the street:
Between the buildings old men talk of rain:
Rain in August and the silver dust is splashed upon the pave
Rain on the fruit stalls, on the grape-man, on the orange,
The organ-man huddles under a sagging awning,
His painted parrot ruffles his feathers:
Goodbye   goodbye

Taxi horns drift by
Shall we walk forever in the streets
Shall we walk forever under the awnings
And emerge to rain falling, and wade through
The green lights without remembering
Why we are here?

THE DAYS GO OVER LIKE WHITE FLOCKS OF BIRDS

The days go over like white flocks
Of birds who never waver
But pass one flock behind another flock
In great streams:
And yesterday M. Milhaud came down into the basement
With sunlight on his shoulders
And dust in the worn spots and his ears very red:
It is snug and black here in winter
Like an adder's hole
And green slime will grow on the walls
When the weather is all rain:
Outside through the branches of seaweed
One sees the people moving in the watered air
One may float to the opaque window holes
Under the drowned land:
They will number these streets: turn to the left
Beyond the corner where the blue buildings swim:
Brown brown brown are these winter days
And smoke moves in this light: wood and cigarette:
And tap tap and clack clack go the feet the feet the feet:
Suspended above gardens and watching out the days
She takes a cigarette and the smoke streams up
Between her leaf-green eyes
She lifts the mouthpiece and laughs
Oh   Oh   M. Milhaud   Mister Meelhode
They were emptying the ashes into the grey bins
And making a great deal of silver dust
While three children skated in brave circles

Around and around in the air
And strings of sunlight unraveled on their heads
Around and around:
The cocheros are brave men who sit upon the high seats
And say *donde   donde*   and clack their long whips
And we say *por alli   por alli*   not making them understand
In the decline of the year the most fortunate things
Come about: and we went sunward and sat on bright terraces
While mother was polite   Oh indeed yes
But laughed so seldom:
Arriba   abajo   does the señora like the alcove
Quiet for dining alone with a child
Arriba   abajo   seeing the courtyard
We will take the bright room here, señor, toward the mountain
She set up a small easel and drew a sketch of me
While I read a book:
But now the season changes: beyond the blue air
The days stream forward forward
We are whirled and brought to this place again
The same pigeons go round and round again
Looking different:
And the children skate past the corners
And appear again in funny caps saying *last one a nigger*
And *race you to Parker Street*   and   *on to the lane*
The first one   the last one:
Snakes in the mountains have gone down down
The snow descends toward the towns
Last month on the distant ranges and now the peaks
Of Silver Mountain   and now Rabbit Hill
With every snow the snakes go deeper
Aspens nod and bow   blown by the wind
And the wind grows colder and colder:

It is not sad   the red hills stand out between the rows
Of colour with bright rocks half way up and at the summit
The roads frozen over
The snakes burrowing deeper:
But it is all different from what I dreamed
It is moving moving
The days pass around and around in the air
Like fragile birds
And with my head turned downward I see
Only their shadows pass on my hands
That are motionless and dead.

STREET SCENE IN DECEMBER

She sits behind the window glass
She is sewing on hard cloth:
The lights in the other rooms go on and off:
The darkness shudders.

And the streets for miles become
Windy and black: they are soundless
And no one steps in the snow:

I pass beyond the street called seven
And enter a doorway and feel that I am welcome:
The lights go on the room is warm
The darkness shudders:

You light the fire and throw the windows up
The man in five is playing and the piano notes
Drop downward and the flowers
Brought in yesterday are wilted:

We see there are no figures walking
And my own footmarks fade where I rounded the corner
Coming to you out of evening:

No one else steps in the snow.

EVENING TOWARD THE STREET OF FERRIES

I walk toward the street of ferries,
And above them westward there is the sky
Colour over colour
And then the low long barges
With their pink and blue tiles float along   float along:
Do you remember the barge we knew in that river?
It was blue and had the sunlight on it always
They were to sink it but before that
You went down in the early morning to make a sketch of it
And later that day they sunk it by the great rocks:
Beyond the window a woman with an old grey face
Startles a little: the jaw moving moving:
The eyes and the street: air between: a window pane:
Could I offer you a handful of pigeons?
They circle the brave housetops
Their ballet conjures up dreams and visions shared and
        remembered
Evenings linger now beyond the windows:
Arms leaning too long bear the white circles outlined by red
Imprints from the window-ledges:
Lighting the candle she waits: she is true to her kind
She stoops to the piano when she hears:
Her wrists are delicate: below her sleeves her hands:
But upward upward toward the street of boats creeps a
        coloured fog
Dominating a lost sun and mounting into the streets
Where children turn and dance:
Low strong fog whistles sound, foretelling winter

In somnambulistic tones
So that all above the ground and all beneath is shaken
Over and over:
I take the curious brown street foot by foot
Foot by foot   the circles
Go round and round like a dance.

YOUR BLUE MOUNTAINS

Your blue mountains were fruitless
There were too many snows
I slept in the night awaiting a lover
When he did not come I knew it was morning
I went into the streets among the people
They were walking to the cathedral
And they went in and bowed their black heads praying
I felt sadder than ever
It began to rain over the stones on the dead people
And the flowers lost their petals
But the trees looked brilliant
When the sun returned again suddenly
You could see the bones in my hand
Lining the shadow
Too many people have died in this house
Perhaps you had better be moving.

CAFE SCENE AT SUNSET

The blue-eyed boys in the German section
And the Spanish boys with the beady eyes
And the voices and the voices
We are speaking too rapidly
The blue gull and the green water
Are now the green gull and the blue water
Sunset and our table by a window
And Spanish boys with rapid voices
And the bright Americans staring at the mountains
And their sweaters orange and blue
And the girl in white feeding the pigeons
At the church of Saint Joan
And the table and the salad rolling in green waves
And wine the bitter wine
No water no goat's milk
Will you have an absinth
We will not have anything
But the sunset in the glasses and sunset on the plates
And rapid voices and voices and voices
Some of them are beginning to sing.

CANDLELIGHT

Now when I take my hand away
There are the lilies
And the gay heads of ladies
And swarming over the translucent bowls the pale gold wine
And at the window the curtain blows and blows
The green deer has run and tasted water
And now he grows wider and his head is longer
On the light wall
Now darkness begins to drown us
And the candle goes down
And we plunge our arms handless to lift the yellow cup:
Your words are not clear:
They go down as our hands in the blackness.

THIS CITY

This city is windless sealed within mountains
And in the valley there are floors of flowers
And ice-slides on the hills
And beyond that blue
A glacier bent like a cup
And rocks:
Look, the blackness is sealing the city
And is windless
We are afraid to talk
We walk through the streets between the taller buildings
We turn
We take hands
It is better to go to our lighted rooms among the breathless trees
And sleep in the suspended silence
To hush our footfalls
And bind up our dreams
Than to walk in such a city
And all the people dead.

INSTRUCTION FOR DREAM

The metal has gone from the sun
And all the streets are lightless
Soon you will be coming
Your footsound will echo slowly
On the stairs as you come
Upward upward to me:
Speak in a softer language
And hushedly:
The room trembles as the roar of traffic grows:
The gown is yellow and golden:
There are black flowers on it
You lift my wrist to your lips
And where you touch it the blood comes out
And soon the mark is colourful:
The streets will forget me,
The doorways will have others,
They will go away,
And this movement
Will carry over
Stars and fragments of sleeping:
I think there will be bright music:

And you will rush out and be carried
Through the evening,
Voices and sounds and figures
In the stream which drowns you
Will not impress you
Will not have any meaning:

You will lie down in the strange bed
After the journey and the cold will cover you
And the bright form of dream:
And this movement will carry you over,
As it carries others
As it carries me.

LAST LETTER

The dream has gone under:
I have returned to where the cedar hills
Wear darkness for a crown:
I have returned and come upon
Only darkness and a stone.

The dream has gone under: sun
Now is black: where cedars were
Nothing now: where birds were
Nothing now: no sky nor day
But only whirling cold oblivion.

I have come back to cedar hills
And bitter winds that seize
The lines of mountains, and bend
The branches of the greatest trees:
This is the end:

Under stone and rock and leaf,
Under wind and tree and hill
Only blackness creeps and kills the brief
Hours over: and this is the way we went
But every stone and leaf was different.

REMOVE THE YELLOW SWEATER

Remove the yellow sweater,
And listen to the late thunder,
And across the street, the mechanical piano
Playing: The Red Red Rose.
Monday evening and the wine glasses are half empty,
Last night the books fell from the mantle,
And today the flowers died in the blue bowls,
And I sent them away in an ash can painted silver.
Does this remind you, then, of nothing?
Are you not reminded of everything
Standing at once in separate colour,
Waiting for a long night,
And a double row of candles,
And old women crying loudly in their black shawls,
And old men blowing their red noses?
Do you not see the signs are out,
The blood pool in the street shed by a signal light
That does not turn to green again:
Children lie down in their laughter and sleep
Little ones drag their dolls of what names
(What names, little mothers?)
We all lie down to sleep suddenly
The cars are filled with flowers passing
With a soft whirr:
This whirr continues to the last street end:
We can hear it faintly.

NOW WE HAVE PUT OUR LONG LIMBS DOWN

Now we have put our long limbs down
Covered in darkness
And cupped our hands upon the sheet
Turned outward:
My breath is closing quickly:
Beyond me lies the night: people dancing:

The sea floating a white moon
And the lake where the boats go up and down:
What do we seek
What are the trees doing
Where do the crimson crustacea crawl in the deathlike night
We have put our long limbs down
Sleepless sleepless forever
We go backward and forward
The ships cry to each other
The stars stand still in the heaven but not so in the water
Sleepless we lie in the pools of darkness
What sort of death do we dread
What sort of death do we wait upon?

PLEASURE ISLAND

We will desert your madness,
We are worn with your gold and glittering lights,
Tired of the puppet-shows, and the lewd mulatto dances,
Moddom of the snake-pit,
And the dwarfs and the illusions:
And the gypsy on the gilded seat
With lives before her in a glaring globe:
We leave the dust raised by the shuffling feet:
Oriental music, and the shrilling calls,
The artificial fruits hung in their stalls,
Wax men giving forth their stilted horrors,
Blue snakes behind the bars,
The bright ball thrown against the walls:
We move among the tinsel miracles:
Here are exotic animals with dust upon their tails,
Excited and fired by too much light:
The sleepy fish are moving less and less:
And here is metallic music: it goes like coins thinly pressed
Together at sharp intervals:
And dust is rising in the light until the air
Takes on a silver look: and round
And round are hung the thousand colours set with light
And noise:
The seekers blink a little
Before they are destroyed
By colour and by sound.

SAN CRISTOBAL

They began in flame these people:
In certain years there were prolonged wars,
And in other years the children died
And women were laid low by grief:
In other times the men went forth
And set a torn flag upon some brilliant island:
A great deal of flame was spent
Before we found this April light upon the cathedrals
Standing in pools of sunlight, and in the shadows thin trees,
And under trees the flowers from warm roots:
We come this April to the lost land
Where no figures move except ourselves,
Where no movement is remembered:
From mountains and the aloof snows
And frozen lakes with their pale flowers
We come and are consumed by thin streets leaning together
In wind, by houses fallen low, spilling their stones
Into their own flat shadows:
The motion of falling blood upon these streets,
The movements of prayers on the lips of the devoteds,
Sounds that rocked here and the bells, are forgotten:
They began in flame these people,
And their motion set forth a short history,
A time that existed and died, and was recorded,
Before they were consumed
Even to the movement of their clocks.

WE REMEMBERED THE POINTED FRUITS

We remembered the pointed fruits
The airs lying between the orchards without moving
Like glass onto which the bright fruit drops:

We remembered and came up over mountains
Out of evenings darkened and moonless,
And the days became brittle:

We left the islands and the walking Fathers
In their gardens, and the church of the
Lady of the Miraculous Medal:

And we went into the black country
Black with rocks and mountains
And the hard faces never laughing:

We went between the hibiscus covered mountains
And the coral floored seas, and passed
The black men standing in boats, returning:

We listened to dice rattle on the flat tables,
And saw the fisher markets, and the boats lined
Waiting for the barges of oranges and coconuts:

Beyond this I know only that we were sent over
As in a dream: and that we have since forgotten
Even the name of our country.

APRIL IN MEXICO

The year has begun to be April
Louis and Raymond
And the skies quicken that were dead
The others have gone walking
People were married today
All sorts of changes but the dead
Raymond, now Louis, will go
Let him, it is April in all the tree-tops, the streets
We will resign ourselves to this sadness, sadness and death
But will return Raymond, everything
The little Russian boy died in apartment ten
Why are they singing
A black window to a black house with black rooms
And all the people are the same as dead
The April twilight dims the sky until there is nothing
All sorts of changes today
People were married
A prince died in a foreign country
Can we never go back
Must we live always in this sounding street
You remark the experiences of the heart are becoming fewer
May be this is death, Raymond,
But surely we will never die, more than this death:
More than this sitting at a wine table without supper
Talking of yesterday, the year being April.

LETTER FROM EXILE

We took the movement
Of fruit growing upon the trees
And the sleepy boats of afternoon
And made them into music:
We swam under the sea-water
And wept in the mornings
And wrote letters,
And at night drank the bright glasses dry
Coming together out of darkness:
We lighted the bright lamps
And were wearied of each other.
It is not this that we wanted
But we have taken the movement
We will follow it to death
Or beyond if there be
Anything after
But you understand
We never meant these leaning seas
To come upon us, nor these heavy days
But now accept them
I, writing,
You understand,
You will understand this.

RAINY SEASON

Heavy rains plod among the hills,
This late season has seen the gradual leave-taking of herons,
The deflected blossoms of the trees,
The sequence of a long and harrowing wind:
In these things a gradual motion precedes the people
Who begin to think of black days within houses,
And the waterbound forest, and rivers become too swift
    for boats,
And the island that will sink three inches,
And great blue thunderheads flagging the horizon.
Thus begins the cave of a nine-months' rain
Into which these people hurry:
Then will the elements be alone,
With water falling, water underfoot on all the walks:
The earth belongs to who will walk among thick mists
Under dripping palms, over broken flowers,
Seeing if he will in the black marshes
The heads of Hydra and the Furies stir,
As shapely serpents pass among the trees.

WATER SONG

One lone swimmer rises from the cooling water
As such figures lift all summer in the river,
In the bloom of water flowers, frightening the swans,
Touching the heavy trees:
The figure rises, and is lost again: he turns
To traverse the long water-path by which he came:
Lightly the soft wind breathes above his darkened head.
He will rise and fall in the water net alone.
The lights of sunset now begin to glow and move
Upon his crystal wrists:
Ankles rise to the surface, and are red.
There is no music swift enough for this.

VOYAGE IN OCTOBER

I will remember you and think on October water
On the sides of boats, and under keel,
Where fast cooling waters gathering their despair
Renounce blue days, and drift slowly where no ships are:
I will go now where October waters garner their despair
    of colour,
And murmur always to the white lands, the frozen skies,
And see on many deckrails your frail hands,
And the imprint of your shadowed head in mists
Where lost gulls wander,
    I will see you on the deck chairs, your hands
Forever still and white, and hear your mind beaten with
    chill music
Returning with October waters to the North, to the white,—
To the frozen skies:
    I will watch (upon the prowrail) under a windy storm
Your hands reach outward to a greying moon when rain comes,
While the colours of a late sea are whirled across the year:
I will go to October's fast red waters, slowly cooling,
And listen to the wheel of gulls' cry, and remember
Your hands, lying on deckrails, and your eyes
Fashioning a heavy music that is never free.

CITY WITHOUT IMAGES

There was a wall about him:
And a blinded city within:
No yellow suns had been there
Only wall and a stone: within
Only wall and stone against sharp air:

    There was an autumn:
    I remember how it came:
    All the air was brilliant where
    Apple trees showered crimson:
    But nothing was the same:

    I remember now: tide's goings
    And darkness without light:
    Everywhere the darkened shore,
    Everything was wrapped in night:
    Brilliance was no more:

    I remember trees were blowing
    Deep in their yellow leaf:
    And then turning and then snowing,
    Plowing the images under,
    Burying the images underneath:

    There was an autumn:
    I can quite remember
    How all bright mornings came:
    Yellow lay on the fields:

But nothing was the same:
There was a wall about him:
And a blinded city within:
No yellow suns had been there:
Only wall and a stone: within
Only wall and stone against sharp air.

THE PEPPER TREES

(1932)

THE PEPPER TREES

It is evening. In the little late rooms the lights are on. They smoke
the sweet pipes sucking gently saying China is a far land. The little
rooms are square and have splotchy lights settling on the fair heads
and the men smile and suck the sweet pipes slowly. Outside the
last light has faded. The street lamps have little power. People are
huddled in small rooms. Children too are in rooms beyond these
thin walls. They have sad sounds in little rustlings that means they
are seated on hard chairs under pools of light trying to make their
lessons come out on the white pages. There are other sounds from
these children's rooms as they drum on the table with pencil ends,
turn a little in their seats to look at each other, turn the pages of
books, spill a sheaf of pages on the floor and scramble down to
gather them up, fold pieces of paper into toys. In the little room
the light falls on the hair of a woman who plies softly on a child's
dress of blue linen. The material is crumpled and new and looks
something like heavy paper with cross lines in it. She says: it is like
the year you went away and sent us the box of apples. It turned cold
slowly that year she remembered and the streets were always filled
with fog and the long sound of boat whistles warning, warning.
Two by two. My shadow falls. Falls on castle walls. On paper. The
paper buildings brought by Christmas have long since tumbled
down. Encouraged of course by Tommy's foot. He said, on the roof,
I'll stand on the roof. And then we cried and tried to build it up
again. We put the house on the grass and said, it is a house full of
ants. They are peeking from the windows. Look. See. Two by two.
My shadow falls. My hair in the shadow stands out. The paper once
white is scribbled over in great joyous circles. Add feet and make
a man. Add ears and make a rabbit. Two by two. Evening. Evening.

Outside the figures walk up and down in the mist, and beyond the corner motors whir, whiz past the light pools and on, blaring their horns, with lovely ladies sitting delicately behind the walls of glass in soft white coats. Over and over the sound of a radio creeps into the street with a sad sad song which is drowned now and then by a boat whistle strong and golden.

What to do all day. Sit inside with fever and think of what is happening. Or what happened at the flower festival the year the boats were filled with lilies and the water was as cool as water just thawed from a block of ice. All around us the cool cool water moved in circles and eddies made by wind, by boats, by hands trailing from boats, wavering under the songs of the people.

Little rooms. Little rooms. She strums on the keyboard of the piano. The light does not take her. Her fingers go up and down pausing here and there without meaning. She cannot play but she is tempted to discover what each key's sound will be. She is tempted and cannot turn back before touching it lightly so that it rings out in a gay little pling pling. The plings do not go together. Her fingers do not go together. They move around each other like two embarrassed people who dare not dance. She wears three metal bracelets upon each arm and they strike together between and with the key sounds. What will she do tomorrow. Southwest winds increasing and rain. Sit inside reading a sensational book with her two little ankles looking at each other wanting to run away. Silver spiders among the leaves creep creep. She knows them in the garden. Southwest wind. Increasing. Suggestions from the pages. The students go into the hall clapping their hands and laughing. One runs behind another with a hand upon his arm. There last year when autumn came. Holidays were the crash of cymbals. Here eyes were leaf green. Dainty skirts. Slim pale hands. Above them, wrists metal encased and musical when moving. He played with the bracelets winding them around and around the flesh. See the circles intertwined with other circles. Round and round they whirled and whirled held by his fingers. We are alone now. The trains roar by. He pushes the leaves about with the bright tip of his cane. The French words go around and around. And it is a song and here and there a note comes up from the piano to supplement the song. Three words and a note, two words and a chord. Treble high and gay. Tomorrow and tomorrow.

And if I am busy or ill on that day I will not be able to come I wrote. But all the same I would like to. But I was frightened. And I turned the black penholder slowly in my hand still frightened. I went in and out between the words seeking some solution. The wind came up. I could hear it in the fireplace where the green stalky wood was stacked because it would not burn. And with a green broom I swept the ashes back. There was the indifferent male standing around with a stiff moustache. He said nothing but the moustaches rubbing together, in the draft of wind said bravo to each other, good morning little donkey, stand still. He cupped his hands and stood quite still and could not hear the bristles laughing under his bright nose. I thought of all drinking men. But my father was never one. Too English. But he had his whiskeys now and then and he gave me little samples. My mother showed disgust and bit her pretty lips. Bravo. Bravo. But my father's moustaches were never loud. They were solemn and brown and bowed politely to each other. When we dyed the kitten purple, the hair stood out everywhere like a flower and he went galloping under the hedge and people in the street said children are so cruel. But when we laughed and ran to get him back we found him crouched under a barrel with his green eyes, now lighter than his fur, full of sparkles. But of course he finally faded and resumed his natural colour. The white mittens made snow carefully into little balls. They were tossed upward into the sky. The sky was snow-coloured too. Smoke came out of all the houses and went up up in strange streams. And on the sled we stuck our legs out straight and played that the sled and we were a spider and then we bent the spider's legs to make the picture real. In one house we passed a woman was playing a piano and all over the white world smelling of smoke there was no other sound but this little tune coming out like a thread and dancing in the snow. We took hands and danced until the song was ended. We waited but after that she played a hymn that reminded me of the cook who whined these dirges every day under her breath in the same rasp rasp and thum thum, rising and falling like that without ever going anywhere. Then an old man with white hair drew down the window shade. The pool was frozen solid and we stood upon the edge in the darkness seeing a steel blue, duller than silver, over over as far as we could see. And moving back late in the falling evening we encountered a snow man who stood like a giant grinning with teeth made of pieces of coal. And we said hello old man where are you going. Ho where ARE you going. And I took his hand. O O the red peppers grow on the jolly trees, the jolly trees, even in winter, even in winter. You remember last year. And the year before. And gay old men brought the puppet-shows into the sunlit streets and we saw them through for three pennies. Ho where are you going, Old Man. Go with us. And we walked down the road holding his hand. Sleeping. Time for sleeping. And we slipped down into the water. O the pepper trees. Even in winter.

THE CITY UNDER THE MOUNTAINS

The wind is strange here. It seems warm and yet when it touches
one it chills. But it still has a quality of fire. On the roadways in
this glaring white hot sun large bottle-blue crabs crawl back and
forth. The native children tie them with strings until they have
a long string full. It looks like a hideous necklace for some mad
queen. I cannot tell you what is in me. I longed to escape from
something. It seemed a tightwalled world enclosed me and that
I might take departure leaving only a shell behind me. I have left
you in the shell. And that makes me know that it is not a shell but
is still a world with happenings incidents accidents deaths. And
when I know the world is there I feel that I have not escaped it. I
see you walking through the streets with the thin sunlight on your
great head. You are taller than the other people. You stride down
the streets avenues parks with a book in your hand. What book? I
sit here writing from a steep house on a narrow street. It is one of
those old Spanish houses and I sit in the window looking down
at a squirming life which eddies about me thick and hot. And
beyond that I see the taller mountains. I cannot tell you how these
mountains look to me as I write. They are blue and high and the
whole city here is blue and high. And on those mountains there is
hot hot sun and yet the snows stay there the year around. And the
equator is not far away. In the mountains there are no roads save
a few trails in the nearer ranges made by the black feet of these
savage Indians. And no one has ever gone to these mountains.
They are utterly strange. And blue. I look at them. I am thinking
of you, without writing to you. We are never able to share these
emotions. It is an error to attempt to. So I hold my body together
tight, wrapped in a bright wool dress, one of those beautiful brown

and white ones that you have liked so much; and somewhere in my body is this feeling I have as I look down into the noisy street and then on past the stone houses to the blue blue mountains. On my table the skeleton of an orchid lies outspread with delicate veins the eye can hardly trace. The stem is brown. It has been dead nine days. It is a delicate colour like fine paper that is very old. I have a great deal of feeling about this dead orchid. It was blooming in a jungle swamp in another country. I pulled it there and brought it with me on the boat. I brought it out of a jungle bog where underneath the boards on which I walked thousands of crabs of every size and colour were moving in a watery ooze. I have never had such a strange sensation as the one of standing just above that mass of brilliantly coloured life. It was never still. The vermillion crabs moving in the black black mud. And others were green and yellow, the exact colour of the leaves and foliage. It was horrible and fascinating. I stood still with that moving sea of bright shells under me. It was dark and damp and insects whirred in my ears and jungle-gnats stung my eyelids until I could scarcely see. I pulled this orchid from a swinging branch and carried it for miles over that perilous bog. There were fires at night along the jungle roads. Fires in the dark, and sudden cries of men from the boats on the rivers that wind between the bogs. Terror. Orchids were blooming, most of them odorless, some of them fragrant only at night. This orchid, now a skeleton, was nourished by rains in a heavy marshland, clinging to the limb of a tree, twisted by heavy storms, dried in the windy season until it appeared dead. It drank water through stems from warm roots. Lived under the heavy days and months, wind and rain. Incessant boom of the sea was near it. The moving floor of crabs beneath. Insects and coiled snakes touched it. It survived the winds, the ants, and the orchid hunters.

I wanted to escape. And here this sense of strangeness is satisfying. Although with it I am holding the thought of you, the two sensations pressed together in a tight oneness. Why do I hold the thought of you? I have often wondered. You too are aware of me. You have written music thinking that I shall hear it. And I have written poems and stories for your hand. It is delightful that this aloof imagination which binds us together somewhere does not touch upon the personal selves. A slow train mounts into this city and I can hear the resounding whistle. The sun climbs higher and higher until the streets reel with whiteness. And the wind has a curious coolness that is touched with fire. Clank clank go the sounds from the rails and the train ascends. Drone drone go the mutterers walking down the steep street. Pling pling go the fingers of someone somewhere practicing on a guitar. I am alive. I put my hand into this sunlight. I am aware of aliveness. I am aware of this strong sunlight which enters, piercing my hand and leaving a slight shadow under. There are strange odors here. Buried deep are the memories of them. I cannot remember when or if I knew them before. Some of the elements of these odors are familiar. I take the odors, divide them into their elements. I remember this one. That one is entirely new. Lemon. Roses. Soap. Toothpaste. Spanish cooking. Sweat. Strange flowers. Spanish perfume, pungent. Oil. Limes. Human excrement. Rotten fruit. Bananas, especially. Goats. Odors too strange to imagine their origin. I like most of all odors that of limes and of certain woods. Some one begins a quick song. It rattles like seeds in a gourd. It is humorous and the people are laughing. I want to walk into the mountains. Straight. Straight. Without ever coming back.

WINTER LIE DOWN IN THIS STREET

Wind is at this corner. Now. It is greater here and forms a large circle and many little ones. The scraps of paper moving indicate the boundaries of the circles. And here and there a variance.

The kite is broken. Now the string lies on the bed with its drooping tail to hold the wind, and the last shreds of paper, and the little stripes of board that made a kite. Broken. Broken. Pink paper sags between thin ribs. Great torn places reveal that somehow it encountered something other than wind. The blue blanket on the bed shows through. The edges curl around the torn places and here is a spot gone altogether. Wind. Late afternoon. The river. Barges and boats. Cries on the wind. Hop two and skip. Jump. Jump. Or run run run. In a blackened hand is the coiled string that holds the life of the pink paper kite now high against the sky. I will keep your secret. Streets are narrow. Beyond the edges of the roofs one late white cloud is sailing away like a blimp only faster. I will not tell. Red sweater tucked at the thin waistline around one large cool apple. Strong string is let out now and the steps go down the street two by two quick quick like the clicking of instruments used in a dance.

In the windows along the streets of the wholesale flower district one can tell the season easily enough. Here autumn chrysanthemums smell of coolness, are associated with coolness. Like the cold rain that year at the end. Everyday in the street without stopping heavy and cold. And at night the fog horns from ferry boats pushing about in the rain on the deep rivers. On twenty-seventh and twenty-eighth streets near sixth avenue the windows are filled with flowers always. One kind or another. In late winter they bring the dainty buds, symbolic, we think, of spring. In summer roses. In autumn asters. Rust coloured chrysanthemums. Blood red dahlias. In the winter hot-house flowers. Lilies for weddings, orchids for evening, common violets, red tongued poinsettias meaning the holiday season. Always one will find the huge tubs of flowers there. Then small flower-vendors set up little displays in every nearby street selling the cheaper flowers for a few cents a bunch. And the wind here, too, whirls and whirls and the flowers from the sidewalk vendors give off sweet odors, while those in the great tubs are behind the thick panes of glass safe from the fingers of the wind. They are stiff in their perfection and as cold as ice. Here, too, is wind. Whirls. It goes round and round the poles supporting the store fronts and round and round the girders supporting the El. Stems. Leaves. Petals. Colours. Flowers wholesale. Flowers wholesale. Flowers.

The wind blows the old skirts up. Ankles and cotton none too clean. But last year. O evenings, holidays. Delightful fraud. Papers crinkle crinkle. Buy. Buy. Evenings and holidays. The jaws click clack together moving the artificial plates of teeth under the horrible skin. Buy. O buy. The hands curved like all the greedy hands in the world. Buy. Buy. The horrid skirts, rancid. The horrid shoes, with broken heels. Buy. O buy. Evenings and holidays. Delightful fraud.

The long El trains creep creep between the street. High enough, just high enough to see in the second floor windows. Hats for a carnival night. Paper flowers. Shades drawn. Novelties. Glassware. Buttons in the late sunlight. Factories for beads. Green yellow amber red blue black white. Sizes and shapes. Young and old. For throats, for the expanse between the hat and collar. Hands move over these beads. Beads move over these hands in the strong sunlight. A girl stands in a window with a huge face pulled into nothing. Lamps made. Lamps designed. Shades of every colour from expert hands. Fingers out and in. Costumes, masks. Pageant or theatre. The artificial gems strike the cold air with vigor. Everywhere the air is ablaze with their strong fiery lights. A clown's head without eyes. Mask of a rabbit head. Gloves for a giant, long shoes for a clown. Spangles for lithe bodies. Wigs red and purple. Wind is up now to the poles on the tops of buildings, and here and there above the city a wilted flag watches, and waves and waves to all the other flags who bow and wave back. The sunlight is strong and slanting. The hour is ended. The school boys wave, until tomorrow. Evenings and holidays. Sundays. Sunlit mornings.

The universe is tossed from a fourth floor window. Catch. O catch. The silver balloon released from a sour faced mother in the hall window of a tenement, glides slowly down where it bounces and then settles to the street. Suddenly the wind. After it. She is gone. She has now in her hand the silver globe which is so light. So exciting. Play it is a ball. Then the wind. She now holds this sphere against her pink face. The two colours are sharp. Her breath comes fast. She is about to know something. She has that O O feeling in her throat and her cheeks burn like little pools of fire. Her breath comes fast. The wind blows between her legs twisting the little skirt. Up it comes and down. The thin round legs are quick and her hands are quick and the balloon is quick and the wind is quicker than them all. Her voice sticks in her throat. She lifts from the ground and down she comes again. There are sounds in the distance but they do not affect her. There are children in the street but they do not affect her. She lifts a ringed finger. She lifts a bare hand. The balloon is between them, above them, in them, on the street. Blowing blowing. Quick quick.

We live near each other. We know each other. We do not know each other. The hurdy-gurdy man plays between us tangling his tin music with the wind. I hear it now. You hear it then. It brings us together. It is beautiful that the wind can stretch the music, pull it this way and that. The music is comical and sweet. It sounds like something made by a child. The hand organ mangles a love song from a recent show. It clangs along through two Spanish tunes gaily gaily. Now the man moves the organ to the opposite side of the street. Children scream as he turns the crank and out comes a version of the Peanut Vendor. I think of the sunlight on the hot faces in the islands, and how every man will stand still all day in front of the phonograph stores listening to this piece over and over. It is played at the bars, at the mountain resorts where one drinks the native rum and watches the island below moving in the quick tide. They play this piece on every kind of instrument. Play all manner of gourd rattles and tinpanny affairs to mark the beat. O lazy windless countries lying at rest in the dark blue seas without cares. And the great windless trees flowering and fruiting with small effort. People who have never known anything, who have no memory. They love the heat, and their glaring islands set apart from the world, and unmolested. Why go there, asked the tourist? There is nothing there. True. Nothing, nothing pressed hard against an eternal nothingness which had no beginning, has no ending. They are not primitive nor savage. They are content with hot drinks, hot sun, windless days, heavy pungent fruit, and the Peanut Vendor round and round without meaning. The wind now pulls out the rhythm, the endless round and roundness of that tune. It blows here and there. The organ man goes away. The children scream. Then there is a long quiet. Then an El train goes over sounding like thunder. The wind pulls at this thunder too and gives a distant rumble to his ears. Now it is over. Past. The sound tapers off. Quiet. Then a fog horn blows a long long blast. Windy nights. Black streets. Darkness. Darkness. O winter lie down in this long street. Lie down. Lie down.

We are soundless as we walk. The wind pulls the words from our mouths and we cannot understand each other. Dying. Dead. Dying. Clack. The cane. Clack clack. The cane. On hollow streets.

Wind on wind. Wind sound on wind sound. In the park the dead leaves dance together, dance separately, whirl about in groups, lie still against the foot. Over again. Sad days. Houses with closed windows. To Spain. To Spain. And the boat rocked along. And wind on the decks blew against my sweater, lifted my white skirt. Slept too much. Grew ill. Died. But did not die. Dolphins of dolphin colour. Ill. Dead. Do not die. Spain. Spain. Hot streets and your cool hands. Guide through. I hate the language. Speak. A little more wine. Cooler, please. The hot streets. Spain. Spain. Take my hand. Frightened. Frightened. First time, you know. Take a coach and wander in the sun. Hurts my head. Sun and wine. Speak. I hate the language. A boy, Senora, a leetle boy. But I am not senora. Senorita still. I hate the language. I hate your leetles, your eetas, your fast bright tongues darting in and out your vacant heads. I hate your language. Streets hot. Forehead hot. Dreams at night of running. Dreams of palm trees wounding the air with one great steady song. Sick for my country. Sick for the dream of my country. There was time for the fiesta. A week of it. Hard and brilliant. Noise wound over and under. No escape. Take my hand. Your cool fingers. Stroke your little mustache. A leeta leeta boy. Fireworks shot and falling. Showers of red. Rain of fire. Lift up your hands. Round your head. Dance like this. Slowly. In the steep country no water. Goats. Flies. No wind. The coast shows a blue sea. Take, take my hand. We run. He is frightened. He puts his head in my lap and lies staring at the sky. The beach is filled with swift and eager runners. They draw their thin legs up and jump. One two and three. A game. A dance. And their shadows too go through the games and that adds ten long weird figures to the group. A leeta leeta boy. Cool serpents crawl between the fevered skins of my fine body. I sit calmly feeling them move me. Under me. In me. Ill. Dead. But not to die. We are soundless as we walk. The threads of sentences are blown out of my mouth and curl round your head. The park is filled. The leaves go round and round. Easy. Easy. Dead and not dead. Winter lie down in this street. Winter lie down.

White white over all the city. He wore a white cap and carried a white rabbit half his own size. Woolly woolly. Winter. The wind went gustily about. Blow here. Steel. Stone. Water. Blow here. Flesh flesh flesh. Blow here. Voices. Woolly dummies whirled on the iced pond. Dummies named with woolly names. Mittens out of mama's pockets. Go to sleep dream. Climb a steep hill and down we go. Go to sleep. Dream. Climb a steep. There. Now. Dream.

UNCOLLECTED WORKS

(1927–1933)

TO A FRIEND

Houston Post-Dispatch, June 13, 1926

This is a love that shall not die—
There shall be no calmness at the last
We shall be spared to weep and sigh
Over a long fled past.

We shall be spared the strange tears
That lovers know—
We shall not have to bear
The shadows of an after-glow.

For ours shall be a climbing song
That none shall guess—
We shall not burn and long
For deathless happiness.

TO A SINGER HEARD TONIGHT

The Oracle, 1927

Your eyes
Were black stars
That rebelled
Against
The songs
You sang ...

LINES FOR PARTING

The Oracle, 1927

So, close the book
That is called "You and I",
The words may never be erased
Though they have no meaning—
And the two brief chapters
Are dead.

SONG FOR FORGETTING

The Echo, July 1927

If it is that I
Never see your eyes
Again—
Nor touch your hand—
Nor call your name
In my soft voice
With tender cadence love has given—
It is then . . . some day
When the sky is a
Blue shell
And the wind a
Vivid streak
Across my hair
My face—
And there is another lover
Of later dreaming—
Think you then
I may
Destroy
Your eyes
With
Infidelity?

SYMPHONY IN BLUE

The Echo, July 1927

Tall mountains where
dim mist lingers—
flowers coloured
out of sky—
winds blowing
over these
somehow, too,
seem
blue.

LARGO

The Echo, July 1927

Slowly the sound of lake water
dies like a music
and the wild dark clouds
that above us are passing
shift to a dream pattern
in black and white movement—
and wind song is low
where the swan heart
sleeps!

SONG COMPOSED OF A DREAM

The Echo, July 1927

Though the
night is a black shawl
across the shoulders
of all sleeping
cities . . .
and only you and I
alone
are waking
far parted . . .
though all seems lost
and dreamings
futile
I have kept the
whiteness of your
face
against
darkness. . . .

SYMPHONY IN WHITE

The Echo, September 1927

Mists
sun
illumined—
mountains
with
snow—
water that
breaks—
a violet
under a leaf,
white, too.

WE WHO HAVE TOUCHED HUMAN SOUND

Free Verse, Autumn 1927

We who have touched human sound
and felt human pain
and gone in swift flight of dreams—
sometimes at night when blanket folded sleep
lies on our limbs like darkness's cover
we in that moment sense
the utter loneliness of death—

GREENVILLE, N. M., MAY, 1927

The Echo, October 1927

Over the tragic tan wastes miles longer
    than the world should be
Incessant winds have taken the water
    from the clouds and blow dry
Cotton balls over the sky.
The cloud shadows that pass over the old
    grey houses free
The earth of glare where brown cattle
    stalk the sun
And the incessant winds continue to run
Over the wide tan wastes farther than
    the eye can see.

MEMENTO MORI—FOR A POET

The Oracle, 1927

She went quietly
and sang
in lonely places.

MEMENTO MORI—FOR A BAD GIRL

The Oracle, 1927

Laughter for her
lovely lips—
pain and pleasure
for the whiteness
that falls
now
into
dust.

MEMENTO MORI—FOR ONE WHO LOVED QUIETUDE

The Oracle, 1927

Death was a lulled dream
hushing the
last sound sound—
the wind seems
to whisper
above
his
lone
grave.

TRIBUTE

The Gypsy, December 1927

I love you
For that fragment—
None of us
May be born
Quite
Whole . . .

MOTIF

Foot Prints of Verse, Jan/Feb 1928

You are a crystal day.
You are a transparent glaze over earth.
You are a frosted glass, shattered and broken
By the dark fingers of Twilight.

COUPLETS PENNED WHILE WATCHING
THE POETRY EXHIBITION

First National Poetry Exhibition, 1928[1]

Grey hair, and shimmering eyes like pools—
"These are not poets, but vulgar fools!"

Thin wan fingers . . . coat sleeve well worn:
"In my heart brittle dreams, have also been born."

Snap and click-clack with brilliant scarlet heels;
"So dis is de way a Greenwhich guy feels!"

Old and ben and eyes grown dim:
"This one here is almost like a hymn!"

Slender features . . . hungry searching eyes:
"He who talks of this beauty, only lies."

Sharp nose and dry chapped skin . . . drab hair;
"Twelve years now, I had held the principal's chair!"

Collegiate . . . dapper . . quite the latest style;
"I write poetry, too . . . You'll pardon this smile."

1. Inspired by artistic salons in which a jury of one's peers decided inclusion, rather than a lone editor, as was the way so often with poetry, Lew Ney and Ruth Widen, friends and correspondents of Kathleen, would put on the First National Poetry Exhibition, which resulted in a scrapbook that would be exhibited in libraries around the country. It was at this exhibition in San Antonio that Young would meet Charles Henri Ford, at Lew and Ruth's recommendation.

CAPRICE BURLESQUE

First National Poetry Exhibition, 1928

To pursue the mad illusion of dreams
and of love
knowing all the while what life is
what death is
what these things are
this is like striding too long
and losing balance.

To pursue the mad illusion of your lips
and your love never proffered
knowing all these moments what we are
what dust bodies are
what limited walled prisoners
we are within our dream shadowed ego-cage
this is pirouetting on toe-tips
and falling to awkward pain.

To press forward in the wake of your beauty
and your body's beauty
diverted long ago
knowing all the while what an echo passion is
what a disappointment a lover's body is
must be
what stunted little animals we are
crying sex in the dark night times
this is trying to leap too high
to sudden music
and falling to the reality
of fractures.

CLOCK-TICKS

First National Poetry Exhibition, 1928

The clock ticks laugh together
over this heart break
they murmur after their laughter
about time . . . and seasons . . .
and quick death that ends in rotting in the grave.
They laugh and murmur together
knowing that time is fashioned of unreality
that life is a solemn breach between two deaths . . .
hiding their laughter and their murmurs
behind the shadow of the face . . .

Time is only a little breach between two deaths . . .

We wait here for the time to come . . . to go away . . .
to bring a new lover or to crush the sight of him from our eyes
or to bring a gown of golden cloth
for youthful slenderness . . .
some of us wait for death . . .
Time will come . . . and go away
but his footfalls are quieted
that none may hear . . .

We wait for time to come . . . to go away . . .
to bring a durable love
or a golden gown
or a sleep that spends away
this silence.

These songs are about time . . . about clock ticks . . .
about silence that is stilled unto the dark robe of death.

There was a year
There was a point in this year
that belied time.
there was a month . . . a day . . .
a perfect moment . . .
a point that has receded again
and left pain and wonder . . .
there was a month . . . a day . . . a moment . . .
passed now like a noontime shadow.

Men's voices jaggled back and forth
the sound falls in my window . . .
a car leaves a trail of sound
falling in with these . . .
life so important
this day so important
a bubble in the dark pool of a million unspent years.

I was one with solitude.
I was one with a moment in time.
I was shoveled in a deep grave.

Flowers are wheels of fire
crimson . . . vermillion . . . scarlet . . .
bleeding against other flowers of blue . . . azure . . . sky color . . .
petals fall at the vase foot . . .
cover the clock with colors . . .
protesting what death is . . .

protesting what beauty is in the point of time . . .
time whirls . . . petals drop . . .
sound is a running figure
wrapped in blue smoke
falling over the autumn trees.

The trees have a golden light running through them . . .
soon it will cover the greenness
it will trace out every mark of summer.
when the yellow veils have been shorn
the trees will grow stately
and robe their grey limbs with shawls of canescent snow . . .

But when the winter has frosted the mood of this day
time will remain to haunt forever my heart beats
to pour clock ticks and clock laughter
into the indefinite wound of myself . . .

Time is only a little breach between two deaths.

EVENING AT THE WATER'S EDGE

Dallas Morning News New Book Page, February 5, 1928

The herons cry over the blue water,
The ducks ride the waves beyond the white-sailed skiffs,
And the fishermen turn their boats to a dim shore-line.
For a moment the air is liquid blue and rose,
While the sun between two towering dark night clouds
Drowns slowly out of sight.

POEM IN BLUE AND GOLD

Parnassus, March 15, 1928

You meant
Cool blue linen
Jean, you meant gold hair,
You mean nothing now, who walk
    beside this
Blue sea.
And this gold hair above your head
Means nothing, now,
And you, Jean, who walk
Mean less
Than one pale gold shell beside this arched
Blue sea.

EXHIBIT NO. 29—NOVEMBER WATER COLOR

The Echo, April 1928

The stream
Is a green curve
Following the willowed course
Dragging a slow net for scarlet
Birch leaves.

TWO

The Echo, April 1928

They say on the pier end,
Their thin legs dangling toward the blue water;
They rocked their thin bodies
In rhythm with the lapping waves against the boats.
They had hard cheap eyes like fragments of dark glass
Set in their elaborately dressed thinness:
This ain't no place to pick hansome gents
But they kept sitting there,
Rocking together with a rhythm.
They were there when the night fell down—
Staring at the water.

AIR FOR A MINOR STRING

The Echo, April 1928

I saw her beauty, luminous as a star,
Her heart where the beginnings of strange dreams are.
I saw her body, lucid in one moment as lone
As a white gull, that lies now beneath a stone.
These are the things I think of, and it seems
The image grows more real; these things, they say, are
　　only dreams.

ILLUSION

Visions, May 1928

Once more we shall sit within this room
And stir our thoughts to speak some word.
And quietly through the deepening gloom
Shall a fragment of each heart be heard.

We shall sip flame from a glass
Of iridescent petals; we shall say:
"Lovely, yes, but this must pass,
This is the prelude to a barren day."

CLIMAX

The Lantern, May/June 1928

What things I knew
Have worn my heart bare:
Here is the feast for you . . .
Pull up your chair!

VIRGIN

Southwest Review, Summer 1928

For Lois

You would feed your fierce desire
From my lips, with white fire.

But I have no keys
To these strange mysteries.

Why will you in urgency press
Against my fragile loveliness?

I hold no key
To this mystery.

HUNGER

Opportunity[1], June 1928

For Preston

Your body is a dark wine
I lift to these trembling lips of mine.

Your body is a harsh dark bread
Broken that my hunger at last be fed.

At the end, this dreaming fantasy
Shall let my body and soul go free.

1. *Opportunity* is subtitled "A Journal of Negro Life". It is very likely that her work's appearance in this magazine—which featured poets of all races— that led to speculation that she herself was African American, a claim that was repeated in university archives as well as Wikipedia until recently.

DIVERTISSEMENT

Palo Verde, Vol. 1 No. 3, 1928

Take your golden head off and place it in his lap
Take your body and give it to a fool;
These passions that consume your dreams
Shall lie as lightly as your body in a pool.

ALTERNATIVES

Palo Verde, Indian Summer, 1928

To see you again and let my pain be known,
Or shall I, into some far alien land,
Bear this heart thing, heavy as a stone,
This hunger you can never understand?

Or shall I paint my lips, and wear my heart,
My unbecoming heart, upon my sleeve,
Playing the old role, the self-same part,
That nothing, even friendship, can retrieve?

Or shall I go at midnight, and transcend.
Like candle breath, some stairway of the wind?

OF A DREAM[1]

Palo Verde, Indian Summer, 1928

For Charles

Down where the pools of his eyes are
Down where the blue pools break,
I go crying in the darkness toward a star,
I go with weeping for a new love's sake.

Down where the blue pools turn at night,
Where the lily roots have whitened arms,
I have in this swift moment gone, in flight,
Spending my beauty for these ancient charms.

Now I fear, returning to this virgin bed,
And I, no longer crying, from this new brink
Come and lay me down like one just dead,
Remembering without solace, pools where bright dreams sink.

1. The poem was also sent to Charles Henri Ford in a letter dated March 1, 1928 following their first meeting at the Carnegie Library in San Antonio.

PRACTICAL

American Poetry Magazine, September 1928

Pegasus has fled—
Leaving me for this journey
A donkey, instead.

Pegasus for flight—
But this one is slow and sure
For travel by night!

SEA'S EDGE

Troubador, Autumn 1928

One heron's cry calls
the round crimson sun for dawning;
And the shell strewn sand
under the white edges
of the ragged water
keeps murmuring your name.

DREAMER

Troubador, Autumn 1928

I am the nourishment
That makes the gold leaves glow,
I am the food so spent
That roots may grow;
I am the dream, that ending
While the cold moons set,
Vow to keep dreaming,
Mending the silver net.

ELEMENT

JAPM, September 24, 1928

I am part of all that I have seen:
White mornings, starred noons, and sleeping seasons
Broidered with silver and crimson, and lean
Long winter days with mocking blinded suns
Gone dead with cloud shadow, when the first snow
Fell like a thin white veil upon the earth;
These I have known, and moments, and the glow
Of candles in blue darkness, the new birth
Of flowers thrusting up the April ground,
And lover's lips as dark as roses are,
The voices of slim girls in surging sound,
And I have been intimate with one first star.
These were my days, my dreams, an integral part
Of all that you forego of my strange heart.

REQUIEM

JAPM, December 24, 1928

And they shall say: there she lies
With this silver dust for eyes;

Coffin boards to pierce her through,
Fiery blood as bleached as dew;

And none shall say: she has gone
On her stairway to the moon.

ON A DAY OF RAIN

Interludes, Christmas/New Year 1928-1929

The rain is a grey green veil
Dragging the world with sound,
The leaves of the aspens whirl
In a sodden rain pool on the ground.

Day breaks at last with a twilight—
Then softly over the bent summer trees
Blue darkness lowers a light
Cover . . . and white doves sleep under eaves.

LINES TO A YOUNG PRIEST

Skyline, January 1929

His beauty's not for me,
His dark-robed mystery;

Not mine now his white fire
Who has forsworn desire;

Nor yet for me such peace
As his dark eyes release;

Nor yet such quiet breath
As he will know in death.

QUEST

Contemporary Verse, February 1929

For my body these four men
Who shall have me now and then;

One shall wake my sleeping eyes
To some dream-starred paradise;

One shall bring me mad release
From the quietude of peace;

One shall pierce my dark heart through
With a silver word or two;

One shall rob me of the sun
And leave me when the day is done;

For my body, sharpened need
On which these four lovers feed;

But with images I keep
My heart, for a purple sleep.

the world turns and is brilliant now

"Six Poems", *Blues*, February 1929

the world turns and is brilliant now:
see, now the narrow streets reel with yellow,
color is everywhere, sun in the streets,
and wind on the waters under the yellow mists.
down narrow paths the leaves blow and blow,
and winds talk in yellow music.
yellow is over the world now,
yellow winds are, and yellow leaves,
and mists on the river whirl golden with winter sunlight.
sunlight is over and under walking people,
is over under and about children crying in the streets,
all is color that twists about those who are walking,
over and under walking people
this sunlight, yellow winds blowing from the river, and blowing.
see now how the little streets are pools of yellow
where the small people go down and leave but a yellow circle.

the moon is almost, but not altogether shining

"Six Poems", *Blues*, February 1929

the moon is almost, but not altogether shining,
and little streets are dark with certain shadows.
beyond sharp corners winds break
and brittle leaves follow and follow.
through mists that fill to the brim
these carefully spaced darknesses
that are now known and spoken of as streets,
winds have a knowing way of falling,
winds have a sweet in no way new
or even altogether arrogant or subtle
manner of weaving moods
from these moments in which the moon is not quite
nor yet in any visible manner shining.

I could dissect you now that midnight

"Six Poems", *Blues*, February 1929

I could dissect you now that midnight has mended certain winds,
and now that streets are sleeping, and the only minute things
that are still crying
are the last lips of little crimson leaves.
I could dissect you, coldly, now, saying:
you are (must be) the little sob
the wind has before it goes,
and the little shadow the dark has before it goes,
and the little sound that music has before it goes,
and strangely you are like a shadow broken on a wall.
midnight, now, and blueness. and I, saying;
saying coldly what you are
of the carefully builded nude small things
that you have sobbed against my breast.
while streets are asleep, now, now asleep,
and only the minute things that are still crying
are the brittle voices of dead small crimson leaves.

remembered from midnight

"Six Poems", *Blues*, February 1929

remembered from midnight: leaf sound and rain
and the moon dropping down slowly again.
remembered from the first thing: one shadow
that swiftly trailed a crimson length on snow.
remembered from the new thing: only old
blind days (always the same),

                    spaced time: blue cold.

if moments spaced of ourselves

"Six Poems", *Blues*, February 1929

if moments spaced of ourselves
make, say, altogether lively laughing ghosts
that chatter against time, noisily,
then let us pause, and build in the blue moon dust
that thins the midnight whirling to darkness,
say, each of the other's lips, or maybe teeth,
or of fingernails too carefully polished,
some dark image never wholly dead but sleeping,
and go beyond the first surface
to where darkness is more than a tarnished mirror,
or where maybe we are ever so slightly and beautifully dead.

since the night when we talked

"Six Poems", *Blues*, February 1929

since the night when we talked
snow has fallen over all the streets,
and in the alleyways and over trees,
and fences and houses and gardens
have been whitened and buried and hushed,
and all last leaves have gone darkly blind under weight of ice.
streets are white now the snow has fallen
swiftly into the blue air of afternoon.
men have walked here in this snow,
footprints have been deep here,
winds have traced the snow over,
and children have been walking here in this same snow.
since the night when we talked
snow has fallen over all the streets.

WHO HAD WALKED IN SUNLIGHT

Palo Verde, No. 5, February 1929

Who had walked in sunlight
In a crimson dress
Will now feed on black bread
And utter loneliness;

Who had made the round moon turn
By the gesture of her hand,
Will now know contentment
In a lightless land;

Who once had sought to build
A straight and silver stair
To beauty, is now content
To finger cool dark air;

Who had known bright morning
With a new and yellow sun
Is content now to trace
Her images in stone.

FOR ONE WHO GRIEVES

Contemporary Verse, February 1929

All the grief that will ever be spent
Will know her pale mouth, her eyes;
She has seen her world mirrorwise and bent
Into the pools where darkness lies.

All that is of the dark will cover
Her thin heart, her flesh swaddled bones;
She will weep over and over
Walking on the last dark stones.

When the high world ends and the mind
Gains a new unlimited dark, she will scale
The impossible heights, and the blind
Ghosts of her brain will slowly pale.

LINES FOR A DAY IN EARLY APRIL

Frontier, March 1929

Although the day is grey
And wreathed in tangled rain,
Down under the hill road
Spring has returned again.

Down beneath the garden
White apple trees that bend
Snow, monotonously,
Under the bated wind.

WINTER BURIAL

Parnassus, March 15, 1929

Now in the clamouring coldness
Of the night, the thick
Insensible roots of dark, this
Sound shall grow to a music:

None but the wind and ground,
The thick snow patched on a hill
Will know when this threaded sound
Has grown still.

None shall know:
Roots under the winter wind
Will grow and grow
And weave an approximated end:

The winter night, the chilling dark,
The last dull thread
Of root growing upward will mark
This gravestone of the dead.

INCIDENCE

Cleveland Club Woman, April 1929

Into the upper air we went,
Who bore two dreams,
And love and youth, unspent.
We played with two-edged words,
And both knew fatal wounds
From these bright swords.
The day was blue, and one huge cloud
Came down upon us
Like a thin, white shroud.

SPRING POEM

Blues, April 1929

in the old man's mouth a s e e d   had grown
and in the cold darkness the roots went downward
    in his soft brain:
nothing ever flowered but it all died very sweetly:
and there were   n e v e r   any lilylike children
to pull a pale flower from the old man's head:
the spring came and the   s e e d   was there
and it all rotted   v e r y
               swee t l y

POEM

Scepter, April 1929

The wise are those who die,
Whose bones are thrust
Between the roots, to lie
Thickly sweet in dust;

The wise are those who know
No cold wind sound,
Where dark seeds grow
Deep in frozen ground;

They for the fiercest element
Are proven: whose
Thin bodies are rent
With roots of rose.

POEM

Scepter, April 1929

Say that I do not know
How deep wounds are:
How dark winds may blow
And obscure a star:

Say that my heart
Is a yellowed leaf:
Say that I feel no part
Of any stark new grief:

Say that I am a stone:
Say darkness plies
Only the dreaming grown
Under my amber eyes:

Say this or what you will:
Turn my barrenness about.
Here beauty has grown still
Beyond doubt.

LINES FOR THE END

JAPM, May 27, 1929

And if we reconcile ourselves to this:
To words and glances
That disclaim this love,
Something out of memory will prove
How little the dark will press
Into our separate loneliness:
If then we keep nothing
No clotted words can bring
A thousandth ghost to stalk
The hollow margins of our talk.
Then will all beauty be thrust
Between the lips like rotted dust!

SHEAF OF IMAGES

Blues, May 1929

Like a sweetly new white shell,
And like music under an ocean,
Under waves and blueness: rhythms and images
That pulse continually and are never still:
Like a new white palely veined shell
Broken to drink of the sea
And the sea's music when the night dies:
Walking on the shore
Dimness lightens and lowers
And a thin gull screams and screams again:
And under all this, remembering and walking
Holding your profile against my trembling brain
Trailing a long shadow behind me
I watch a red otherwise usual moon
Fly upward from waters and accentuate blackness:
And blackness and a light:
And under the shell and the shadows, seeking
To evoke music in a brilliant mind,
Walking over the thousand lives I have been
And having been, and having been,
Continue to run their little courses and recede
Like half noted music,
Night brings no new things,
Only old ones that are somehow connected
With this dream.
Like a sweetly new and marvelous shell
I break you and drink of the sea:

And a tall shadow walks behind me
And asks for food:
And my shadow and I walk, and the waters
Over us, and the waves walk over us,
And the waves, only the waves.

FRAGMENT

Transition, June 1929

Helen will walk queen walk, Helen will walk queen walk through
the insufferable shadows, will walk with all her ashen blondness
saying : no i ain't hard up : and : what ud yuh suppose. Queen
walk. In the slumbers maybe sunshine. Maybe in the slumber that
leaded quality of sunshine. Slumber. Slumber. Between the newest
abortion no one knows anything of. Who has not lived queen in
a basement with many babies. Why all the alleyways are full of
sunshine and Helen queen blond walking in the sunways keeps
thinking of her baby in the hot sunshine. Yes Spring is the sunshine
of queens in the sunshine of queens. Yes Spring is little alleyways
brimming with sunshine. Yes the mountains came darkly. Oh God
how darkly the mountains CAME. Maybe the evening . . . maybe
the night . . . and her mother's screechy voice screaming *kathleen*
while the mountains moved darkly. There was rain later and when
it rained the mountains came down fast like the rain. It rained the
great thick mountains on the door step. Clotted laurel came down
in broken streams. In the gutters the dead laurel lying whitely dead.
The ghost of the laurel and the mountains converging slowly darkly.
And the screaming voice. Helen will walk queen walk. And the
alleyways are sunshine. But I do not understand. But it IS Spring.
And another Spring there was the baby . . . and the other babies . . .
Who had never been BLOND except when kissing Helen. Helen
who walks blondly like a queen over the slight sunshine over
all the things that are newly quickened holding little syllables
of delight between her blond lips. They had said : NO no other
way : you see how the river comes : it is clotted with Spring rains :
you see how the winds come. And all the feet go on pacing and the

feet go on. And walking with all the dark ones SHE the blond
queen tipping little feet and tripping little blond feet over the dark
pavement wearing new panties with lacettes and bowettes and all
the little ettes that fill the hearts of all the little blond queens who
walk over the black April pavements while the Spring means the
mountains coming down and the usual crop of abortions. What are
aesthetics? But she couldn't say because the mountains were so near
and dark : maybe once when the dress she wore was blue : it was
May just turning May: red birds were thick in the blue heavens :
God how blue the heavens that day and how blue her dress : God
how blue her dress when the red birds came and she lay on the
thick red earth that had been gashed by the new rain and all the
big red birds went over and went over and she in blue lay on the
great red earth and saw the birds fly in crimson twos and wondered. Also she had the mountains. The mountains were great and
dark and had great massed rocks. The mountains *had her*. Then on
such a such a day she sought a red gashed gullet and lay down
under red birds and on the warm scarlet earth and thought a great
deal about the blue oh God HOW blue blue dress. What are aesthetics and what are aesthetics? And what is this? The answer was
about God knows how many blonds walking on the thick pavements and wearing some kind of etty new panties some times
called dancesetstepins by the great voluble Jewrish girls who would
sell them in all their chiffon loveliness to little girls who do not
wash their necks except when April IS. But God how they love the
little panties when the Spring comes. There is something great and
good and beautiful in all this when the Spring comes and the dark
pavements dry from the sudden rains. When the sudden rains are
over the sun comes again and the babies are put in the alleyways to
sun. And then the first moon comes at night in an altogether new
and strangely exciting way and the Spring crop of abortions begin.
Little breasted girls sit in the offices palely chewing gum and

carefully etted until the great and huge DR comes in. Oh yes all this is very Spring and very lovely and very breath-taking and exciting as nothing else can be exciting and VERY very ETTY, Oh God it is all so breath-taking! Before the summer will come and flower thickly and hotly all the little blond girls will go breathlessly over the dark pavements and compare every sordid but also very beautiful sexual and other things of interest, notes. Oh this is very like when the mountains came down darkly and the screaming voice began and the blue VERY BLUE dress began its making and the first red birds were showered down from stunted trees. Helen walks like a queen when her throat is choked with the somewhat doubtful tears about *how he has done her oh so cruelly* and how the family watch her and the baby's last cold who has a coat altogether too beautiful to wear, why then the doubtful tears and the sunshine and the blue eyes all will melt and she will see the most beautiful man in a well cut English suit. Oh in the thick moonlight she will not hear the steady ticking beyond all this but it WILL be very sweet and VERY oh so very excitingly new: then with the thick sort of moonlight worlded everywhere and the etty sort of thought lying in her mind this WILL BE just the greatest LOVE OF LIFE and oh the very greatest most beautiful thing that ever happened to any blond girl in the springtime: oh this will be very breathtaking and oh GOD HOW SWEET THE SPRING!

FIRST LOVE

The Houston Gargoyle, September 1, 1929

He said that he would come at four
And now the hours slowly pass,
No footsteps here, no knock upon the door,
And afternoon is blue and great clouds pass
Trailing their shadows on this place.
I snip a thread, and drink a cup of tea,
Or scan a page on which I see his face,
And waiting think up things to say;
At three I don an orange frock,
And brush my long black hair,
And then watching the slowly moving clock
I am stricken dumb at hearing his footsteps on the stair!

A FRAGMENT

Parnassus, September 15, 1929

The rain has stopped ... darkness comes down thickly ... it seems
to pour through the trees .... late winds rage through everything:
that sound of wind and the sound of cars swushing in waters
that has grown deep on the streets ... all sound: all sound ripped
through my sound of trains screaming their whistles going
somewhere .... the garden bends; everything: grasses and trees and
flowers and jasmine white shrubs are flailed by wind movement
.... Life is not sad like this: there is a newness to rain: to silver:
to wind bending like that: like a promise of something: like a
promise never to be fulfilled. Glaring days have the futile solidity
of life: they are blocks of white stone cold and with life ... only
flaring days with white hot head can be blocks of futile knowledge:
people look different then: but silver days when it is dark too soon,
and when it is too thinly cold, these days people huddle or walk
differently.... the wind has a promise ...

NOW THAT MORNING

Tambour, #4, September 1929

Now that morning in the little streets
wakes, and is blue with the fluttering wings of birds,
that we walk slowly through the dawn,
saying: morning should be all brightness:
while over this the grey, and over the grey grey again
a dull sun illuminates a thousand compress atoms
that are pressing their ways toward grey toil:
that we have seen the gulls blow, and the mists thicken,
and the grey morning a little less tedious than death,
futility walking in the streets in a torn black hat
wearing jauntily in his lapel the tiniest dead rosebud:
morning in the little streets
and on boats at sea and on islands at sea
and walking people through the newly dulled sunlight,
walking people through the grey mists
who are but atoms hurrying toward death again:
but for the moment hurrying through and hurrying through:
all waking people going through the greyness:
I say: morning should be brilliant
with orange sun like mornings in April after rain:
saying slowly of your eyes:
morning should be brilliant and mention carefully April
while your threaded smile climbs into my silence
where nothing IS except April and your morning smile:
saying slowly of your eyes as they turn seaward again
where the birds fall and the waters fall
and the grey mists thicken on the grey dull air:

how little lives are lived on dull mornings
and how my ill and little heart
glows faintly something like the silver moon
that is not wholly dead across the right horizon
of the ship's mist:
under your slow sure eyes:

MORNING.

CONTINUED NOCTURNE

The Forge, Vol. IV, No. 4, 1929

Now if you will listen, Beloved,
you will hear the inner doors of the wind
being tapped upon by thin crimson leaves;
and you may see the sullen rain treading a pathway
backward to the sleeping stars;
and if you will come (cautiously, Gold-Head),
listening over your own foot sounds
as you walk down the stair of darkness,
you may hear, persuasively,
the shell of the little moon
dribbling and cracking with disassociated music,
a fixed star-point between our microscopic hearts.

LETTER

Blues, Fall 1929

I know what you are thinking
now that leaves fall,
and crisp moons are arched over slowly cooling hills,
and little gusts of wind
scatter the late pool-lilies;
I know what this thing is that you hold,
the solid hours, the thing you keep
between your mind and body,
brilliant as blown glass, heavy as an iron shaft:
I know the food you taste, still thinking,
the water you drink, devoid of bitter crystals:
I know the sleep you sleep,
it is crimson over valley-roses
dredged to a minute thinness:
I know the mornings you have,
(they never come here)
but there they are turning cold,
and harsh sounds of leaves grate on your sleeves,
pigeons nestle to your fingers,
clouds, over, swinging to your eyes:
I know the slow cool first after-midnight
walking on leaves, talking: "it does not matter,"
the winds, and the leaves, and the dark making it matter:
I know the slow white water,
and the snow later,
and the thoughts that come after white darkness:
I know what you are thinking,

birds to your fingers, and remembering,
and the white hot thing,
heavy and brittle between
the swinging body and the cooling mind.

SONG IN A SEQUENCED DREAM

Scepter, 1929

Let us break through to the outer walls:
Here is the darkness and the dead starlight,
Swans on the pool are mirrored all night,
And music grows slow where the cold rain falls.

Let us go down where the river turns,
And dark long threads are plying the rain,
And the red tree-tops are broken again,
And the candle-point of the moon returns.

Let us go to the doors of the wind,
Treading the darkness, thus, star on star,
Leaving the shell of what we were
Buried beneath the ground where the wet trees bend.

POEM

Scepter, 1929

Smooth her face.
Paint her mouth red.
Place black candles
At her black head.

This is the end:
No more shall her lover
Call her little name
Over and over.

No more shall days go
Like birds in sun.
The moon is now set.
The race is now run.

TO ONE WHO AWAITS BREATHLESSLY
THE FIRST SNOW-FALL

The Forge, Vol. IV, No. 1, Winter 1929

You shall not remember how these long dark days were,
you shall not remember these barren walks,
these streets reeling with dead small leaves,
nor how the shadows killed the pale sun at noontime.
you shall not remember these dark grey mornings,
and empty evenings that are cold without the solace of cold,
nor how the dark trees stood in wind.
you shall not remember waiting for something,
and waiting.
you shall not remember spaced grey things
when the first snow, softly, falls.

CONSIDER, NOW

The Forge, Vol. IV, No. 1, Winter 1929

Consider, now, my lady, delicately,
and thoughtfully, such things as afternoons,
such things as roses,
that are not unlike your lips.
and delicately, now, think on rose-buds,
and blue afternoons starred deep with fragrance.
and consider now, my lady, such music
as I weave to you from afternoons and roses.

ULTIMATELY

The Forge, Vol. IV, No. 1, Winter 1929

I think at last I shall have peace,
I shall not run this long cold way of dreams,
Nor rhyme such brittle words as these
To ask what death redeems.

I think I shall know peace enough
To go like little whitened ghosts that walk
The margins of their minds, and snuff
Their brief and fragile talk.

Then this shall be over, swift wind
And dark wreathed pulsings of my purple blood.
Let love and dreams and all descend
To dust, that I may find where beauty stood.

SONNET

Frontier, January 1930

Here where we sit in frail polite chiffons
We talk of how afternoon has roses,
Cut in the thick blue bowls, how afternoons
Will go in straight sophisticated rows
Of days. Tilting our bright and polished heads
And tapping with our slippers on the floor.
We listen as the dark and surging threads
Of conversation heat the wall and door:
A wavering voice lifts, and then recedes
On some brittle crimson note of music:
We grow quiet, admit no older needs
Who have been stirred by slightest magic.
Here we will sit through long dark afternoons
Stifling our hearts between the frail chiffons.

Here the flat earth

"Three Poems of the Southwest", *The Golden Stallion*[1], 1930

Here the flat earth
Unknown to trees
Stands deep in the yellow sun
And the falling houses crumbling to dust:
Here now the yellow grass
Dead in the root last year
Nourishes a thinner newer sound of wind.
Here now the deserted land
Waterless and dried
Driven by a dull barrenness
And unknown to trees
Holds fast with the elements
Where the dry dark has disintegrated roots and bones.
Here now the thick hot sun
Wavering on the small grasses, dead at the root last year,
Will stir and move like a ghost without sound.
There are no shadows here:
The Spring brings no green,
Brown cattle stalk on the waterless land,
And birds at certain seasons
Scream and pass over.

1. Full title, *The Golden Stallion: An Anthology of Poems Concerning the Southwest and Written by Representative Southwestern Poets.*

This is the land; the long red earth

"Three Poems of the Southwest", *The Golden Stallion*, 1930

This is the land; the long red earth
Peopled by some darker race
Who have sat in the sun too long:
Here is the land
Where roots have long decayed
From the mouths of bitter seeds:
Dust and the red earth
And the thick dead grass bending for miles:
Here no shadow has ever fallen,
And the birds go over all day
Screaming.

Here on the dead land the dull grey houses

"Three Poems of the Southwest", *The Golden Stallion*, 1930

Here on the dead land the dull grey houses
Where the roofs cave slowly in the sun:
On certain winter days
Thin figures trace out red paths, slowly:
The bleak houses continue to crumble
Standing in high sun,
And on the long land
Peopled by thinning figures,
By a dark woman and a light man,
The sun whirls slowly on forgotten roofs:
The figures have forgotten what they knew:
At evening scarlet fowls pierce silence, darkening blue,
And the smoke drifts into the pale sky:
They have forgotten the thunder of rain,
While the long strings of the thick wind
Make minor horrors of the night.

LANDSCAPE IN SPRING

The Golden Stallion, 1930

Through sunlight silver birds are sifted,
And broken rotted hands have lifted
Crimson flowers from the dust:
Now the piercing thrust
Of sound from a dove's mouth,
And winds from the mountains: and in the south
Waves pale upon an empty sea:
Wait: in this immensity
Such unfolding brilliancy will find
Clearer mirrors for the minds.

Through sunlight silver birds have lifted,
And crimson petals have been drifted
To the grass:
No more: we are the last who pass
Through all this splendor, having died
Before, and having known before the wide
And brilliant days to go
Breathlessly, row on row:
Weep not if our heads are bent
Unto this bitter sacrament:
Stilled now the landscape where
Everything is drenched in final silver air.

before we left / we made a holiday of water

"Six Poems", *Alhambra*, January 1930

before we left
we made a holiday of water,
blue and cut by arms
we lay sunwise and floating over waves:
we dreamed of far horizons, staring at space
that opened like a tea rose, blowing slowly open.
before we left we made a holiday of water
wind-wise and sun blown without shape
breaking the lucid waters and slight blows:
broken waters: brown under silver
pushing forward to some end:
at last when light lowered someone spoke
and we came back and traversed to forgotten sea:
dust came to our mouths at last,
the taste of sand.

cutting the waves we went northward until the sun

"Six Poems", *Alhambra*, January 1930

cutting the waves we went northward until the sun
had spent: we thought of gardens until the moon came:
we thought, too, of lovers, leaves, palm trees in sunlight:
the moon came splitting our pain two ways:
lips were one, and eyes were another:
and our hands grasping for blackness
taking cool note of water flowing under
went downward until the three foot surface of moon's light
had closed like a black boxlid:
our hands learning of water, went swiftly,
until drowned heads thought no more of gardens
split two wise to eyes and lips.
when the last blackness entered
pools whirled under ship's paths,
and we never returned.

leaves

"Six Poems", *Alhambra*, January 1930

leaves
pressed to my mouth
teaching me strangely, summer in little coolnesses,
say
JUNE is a white lady edged with green,
edged with lover's green,
edged with green lovers,
edged with what i have known:
leaves
pressed to my mouth
have taught me
deathless sunsets sweeping thousand streets,
and the one poignant, before-imagined
taste of dust.

it was just after

"Six Poems", *Alhambra*, January 1930

it was just after
that mary had remembered mothers weeping
and
brushing aside all her sweet gold hair
went down to sleep in the cool river bed:
they found her there three days after,
the sweet gold hair with pebbles,
the thin hot mouth with cold sand,
her head holding the same huge horizon
where no one had walked.

i am troubled at night

"Six Poems", *Alhambra*, January 1930

i am troubled at night:
the tin moon, and the fatted birds,
and the leaning hungry trees, dying slowly under red August,
and the walkers in the streets carrying bundles of words,
carrying whistled music, carrying hands and fingertips,
carrying eyes brimlit, unpooled:
the thin churchspires swimming upward,
and the lonely bells,
and the slight rocked tinkling of voices.
i am troubled at night:
the lean moon, and the slow pondlilies,
the thought of many rivers turning,
of feet walking, a heavy tread, a thick sensed music,
a voice remembered out of passion:
the sun sets for me at the halfnight,
the voices cease suddenly,
and the walkers forget where they are going:
i put forward my hands
and only a silver round lamp
answers me with huge distorted fingers,
and a room with five walls
that are bent and broken.

just after / the staggering sunset

"Six Poems", *Alhambra*, January 1930

just after
the staggering sunset
there was wind:
wind from the w i d e horizons
where there is nothing
we dreamed about in childhood
being just oVer hilltops,
being just oVer grey plains,
being just beYOnd cool gold seas:
there's nothing there
but a save that is dark, unholy,
smelling uncertainly of wind.

CHRONICLE

Pagany, Fall 1930

Here the forever warming waters rock to my door,
and I have set tall candles at night for a conversation
to be held between the lost self
and the one now manifested in my brain:
words come forth singly, or are stifled in their sounding;
the herons come from the swamplands
and sweep their wings before this window:
nothing is forgotten:
      not the sea blue leaf, blue tree,
the trees have the summer,
the flowering of trees that does not cease:
in the morning the sail boats go forth bound for somewhere,
and they return at evening,
and it is with their returning that I light the candles
and the sea comes up between them:
it is then that I think of the lost days of another month:
your face comes up no longer,
      your face returns less seldom
and your hands are confused with other hands:
the tropic days begin to rot away the sentences in books:
I can no longer read:
"Un cygne d'autrefois se souvient que c'est lui"
"With a dead sound on the final stroke of nine,"
I forget all these when the white morning is blown to the sky:
at evening it rains and the skies grow dark,
the rain in the palms sounds all night like
the voice of a woman crying:

it is by this sound, I know that we are lost:
                    sometimes your face rises
half from a dream, and breaks like a chord of music:
I hear the first and third notes, and the other notes are hidden:
there is no more: not even an echo:
at noon I ride to town by sea's edge,
under the banana trees,
here and there the papayas fall with a thud,
often the natives are gathering baskets of coconuts
to sell in sidewalk markets:
herons rise from the jungle swamps
and go forward to other shallow waters:
some of these things do not impress me:
I am thinking and thinking, separating myself from myself:
I see your face before my face,
moving with a thick movement:
I have the certain feeling that we are lost:

          here the flowering of the land
          and I come too late, too late
          the sound of water, and the sight
          of sails at morning, and the trees
          hanging in flower, and the trees
          burdened with fruit, and the long lush
          rain in the date palms: it is over
          and the drought has come upon this land,
          upon this mind, no more the flowering,
          the blood is walled about by fever
          eating out the brain: too late
          the return to the flowering land,
          separating the self from the self,
          the self from the mind:

I have the feeling that we are lost:
it is as if I had run a race in a dream, winning it,
awaking to the same defeat: the dreams in my sleep
become as a muffled screaming, and the dark is full
of terrors: I know that we are lost
when the white birds stand all the dark clouded morning
in the water, in the rivers, and have no voice,
when the rains tear down the flowers
and the sea carries the blossoms far out:
the sound in the palms is the sound
which means we are taken, we are devoured before the sunset:
I know that we are lost: at morning in the coffee cups,
the bitter oranges we peel,
at morning when the water runs cold from the shower,
at morning when we dress:
under the sunless jungle trees the mosses rot:
there is a great deal of decay here:
many things rot, there is a rotting continually:
everything is lost, to be regained,
to be eaten, to be grown again from thick hot roots,
except this self between the self, except the self
between the brain, except the knowledge,
except myself, yourself:
we are forever lost.

WISDOM

"The Literary Lantern", March 16, 1930

Now I find my need has grown
And will not feed realities:
None will measure how a stone
Is thick and dark in images.

Now I found my mind has fed
All too long on sterner lies;
Where a slighter self is dead,
Another has grown wise.

Now I found my want has welled
Until a deepening pool has grown
Until the light has been dispelled
And is dark as undertone.

Rose-root and stone-print
Here where my mind is blown;
Here some stranger creed is bent
Against my own.

Now the mind is thick with sleep
Where images will mark
How wisdom has grown deep,
And deeply dark.

ALL THINGS INSENSIBLE

Opportunity, April 1930

I envy the sleep
Of each cold stone
Where yellow moss
Is overgrown;

I envy flowers
That fall
Their last dark
Burial;

Insensible things
That do not hunger:
Roots that have died
And can not stir:

All things: as stones
And moss and water:
All things that
Do not hunger.

DECEMBER PORTRAIT

Opportunity, December 1930

She now retraces her steps once more
Over the length of the room to the dark window.
She stoops to the ancient piano
And fingers the white keys that pour
Strange music of remembered spring thunder
That she once heard in a youth long dead:
She has not forgotten: she turns her head
To stare into the dark, and hears the winds stir
A new sound: although now vaguely familiar
And yet altogether strange, the chords grow
Crazily wild, and the black window
Rattles, and music continues to thunder:
Some way of sound her dreams may transcend
These stairways of snow, and snow, and wind.

POEM

Pagany, Winter 1930

falling off a fence MARYANN
maryann color of old honey
falling off maryANN
or being seduced under lilacs (maryann)
mating with lilacs:
MARYANN mother of twin black children

falling off no more fences
falling no more

remembering slimly: maryANN color of dead honey,
lilacs, Lilacs, LIlacs, LILAcs, LILACs, till she die.

    the ripe sweet scent of lilacs where they had tricked her,
    had taken the la de do brilliancy of running on fences,
    MARYANN tricked by beauty, dying slowly of beauty,
        maryann,
    color of black honey, dreaming no more.

THE SAD END

Hound & Horn, Winter 1931

We lived in the steep house without gardens but the sun was good
there and the hours heavy. We came to live together promising
nothing and expecting nothing. We came there to work and to
have the sun and to learn again to sleep at night. The house had
steep balconies at the back and in the evening we sat on separate
balconies and thought separate thoughts and the sound of singing
was heavy in the streets. The black men stood outside the wall and
cursed each other in a shrill Spanish, and sound of carriage wheels
and horses' hoofs went on forever beyond the streets. At times I
thought this would satisfy me, and that I could live here forever.

In the streets were flower markets and we saw an old woman
die without passion and these things united us. The trees had roots
and the pulled flowers stood on our tables but we had no gardens.
We often thought we should like hydrangeas and lilacs and pansies
without their meanings. But instead hibiscus buds floated in the
cracked bowls and the hot rooted roses dying within the hour.

We read about snow and talked of living in a northern
country. And wondered if we could learn to ski and speak another
language. In the end we came to say the hot country is good and
the sunlight is healing and it is easy to die here. And
we came to work more and live less and have no adventures.

The end was still more strange than this. She had large ankles
and feet which she placed on a stool beside my own delicate ones.
She remained in bed a great deal and said nothing. Her hair grew
strangely and only the nape of her beck and the tips of her breasts
were beautiful. We felt her boredom added to our strangeness and
in the house I felt that one should not speak unless in whispers.

We had lettuce and apple salad for luncheon.

We drank all day the day he packed his suitcase and made ready to store things. He said *no not for a long time* and *I am not strong enough* and *I must collect my forces*. And I said nothing or else too much. It wasn't sad when we drank and he packed, and we read the papers because it was Sunday. We spoke of an island but never went there.

He said I wanted you to know, *I think you should . . . an hour before you phoned I prayed that you would come back. When I was delirious I thought to come there and look in the streets and inquire for you.* (And we sat on the huge stones and listened to music and the wind came up.) *I thought you should know that after you had called I worked last night, I was able to work. And to-day I kept my appointments.*

He said *I hate this sort of thing*. And he was late rising and we missed the train. He read while the sad train pulled in and out of blackened stations with people alighting and people coming on to their purposes. He saw nothing but that he had stopped the thing that was hard to stop and had helped to be rid of a bad influence.

And she came in with the same train and very silent.

The days grew on us with hot sun and dust on the wild-flowers on the roadways and the clearer nights. We never had each other. There were reasons why we should not and we were a reasonable people. It was different from the first in that much, because there was a consequence and a great deal of suffering, and then the second was different too, and had the fulfillment but no consequence . . . and the third was perfected in sensuous movement. But the house collapsed about us and we saw the hallways darken and dared not speak what we were thinking.

When the car rattled again I knew that they had gone away. I knew they should not come back together and that the situation had come to an end and a very sad end at that.

We thought we heard the thunder shudder through the mountains and under the rivers but nothing came of it. The house collapsed about us and the odor of decaying food crept up the stairway. And when the end came it was sad. He got up to leave, and carried a suitcase heavily strapped and a good sized canvas and a wooden frame that had been taken apart and tied together again. He took my hand and said goodnight and the car rattled off, and the one who took him remained for a long time, and later a train whistled by carrying all of him, his necktie and his ideas, his remembrances and his sense of time. I poured his staling beer out and decided to sleep on a pillow he had used but later threw it off, and slept soundly without dreaming of him at all which was unusual.

The nights became rarer and took up the sound of water and the nickle piano wouldn't play any more and the man in the telephone booth said *I'm all right, the other man was killed.*

He went away to become settled. We settled separately three ways and worked through the night when we couldn't sleep. We had our adventures that we set forth upon and before long became heroes, and were soon after defeated.

The arms from the shallow crowded beaches writhed in hideous motion. We were confronted with deformed torsos and swollen thighs and huge bellies sagging in blue suits. And the music played very loudly and the voices of hundreds of people were loud in it. When we first came to the beach there was an explosion and everyone ran toward the sound. It was a keg of beer and the people were disappointed. On a thin bench two men were kissing.

LOVE STORY

Readies for Bob Brown's Machine, 1931

It was December before we knew it and then January soon after.
We never knew how these days passed and the night seemed to run
one into another with the usual drinking and meetings in the bars
and dancing places wearing soft dresses and laughing.

We walked on the sea walk and stopped on the hard green
benches. When we had stopped we put our arms about each other
and kissed for a long time. It was beginning to be early morning
but it was still dark and no sun. We came for a long way by the sea
and the sound of water and the roar of the wind in the palm trees.

He came into the hospital room wearing a yellow tie. There
were small oranges under my pillow to get the scent of them.
The shutters were closed and the room dark and warm and the
air hugged the odor of dying roses. He talked of the impossible,
saying this thing is impossible.

The man on the corner was weaving a fishnet. Back and forward
and under and over his black hands went and the children were
standing still watching his movements. Oranges were in all the
stalls nearby and roots and bananas and brilliant screaming parrots.

We talked for a long time without getting anywhere. He wore
a yellow tie and held my hand and said I should get well and long
after I saw him sitting in the cafe and the bright girls about him.
He looked impotent, dancing, and unhappy. He smiled to me but
I could not answer him. I wanted to meet his father. It was my way
of getting more knowledge of him and of his country which was so
foreign to me. I wanted to know the very source and root of his life.

We danced in the cabaret until morning and all the tables were
filled with weary-eyed dancers. The bright girls had all faded, Jean,

172 ⎯⎯⎯

and the girl from Vienna, and Conchita who had yellow eyes. Their frocks were a little soiled from the many contacts they were creased from sitting; but the girl were on talking and their throats kept on swallowing the bitter drinks. They had their handbags filled with the little slips which meant that they had made money, but how sad they looked just before dawn and the paint worn off and their eyes too red. We say goodbye goodbye, leave off now, we're going home, thinking of words said to us, thinking of men's hands all of them desirous and some of them stirring. Where is your father? What will he say to you when you go to him this afternoon? He is proud of your small achievements. You laugh together at the easiness of success. Where is your mother? Is she dead? I see the traps laid for you one by one the huge webs while you are laughing. At length we stopped and said goodbye, buenos noches, bon soir, and suddenly it was morning. Goodbye, Jean, goodbye, Angela, the dead, and all the girls in the wilted frocks and stale perfume. Goodbye.

The carnival came later and the streets were hung with flags and flowers and music and drinks were everywhere. During this time we met and spoke and joined hands and danced slowly around and around, without talking. We were a little excited but tired. Tired of drinking laughing dancing, tired of the little cages and the entertainers and the tropical weather. We were so tired and sleepless that we danced slowly saying nothing, but it seemed to us afterward a very splendid ending as we danced to the slow music at the season of the carnival. When the dance was over we went back to our tables smiling wanly.

For days afterward we went along the same ways. The sun shone too fircely and the wind dried the tree branches and swept the trees bare again. There was a rattling on the pavement of huge leaves. They were swept seaward. We could never recapture the mood of those weeks of long nights and days glazed over with sleeping and telephone calls from bright voices. The laughter had gone and we had nothing to say. We met the same people and each other and were speechless. The carnival season had come for many. But not for us I kept this sameness until the boat was seized by the tide, it was sailing at eleven, and I was wheeled in a fog of gulls beyond the days of this island.

QUESTION FOR YOUR QUESTION

Poetry, September 1932

For E. B.

The leaf is stripped from the tree,
Crisp gold at the edges
With brown veins, now powerless
Against the frightening wind.

We took from the dark the terrible speeches,
Syllables into sentences,
The steep sea beneath us:
Where are our children?

Where is our land?

The blank crags at morning
Holding birds and sun:
At night we ventured up
To know the laurel.

Where is our land?

The rose, down now, in water;
The pool reflected on the wall
With the quivering of fishes
Set below and above it:

We two in the park, forbidden,
Asking for everything, asking meaning;
Staring at the crystal

October beyond the white river.
What is our land—mountains, crags,
Snows on the higher ledges?
Islands with birds floating over,
Palms, the land of the plantain?

Here is the garden,
Polite, quivering with sunlight and water,
The little tails of fishes,
The leaves rattling as they move.

Where are they going?
Where are you sitting in this sun?

But if you have this history,
Look, closely—your face, arms, hands
Move in it, over and over,
The record is you and of you,

Is me and of me, containing both
From the days upward
Before and after we ascended
Asking love.

HOUSE FULL OF WINDOWS

Published posthumously in the *San Antonio Light*, April 12, 1933

The winding sound of doves blows in from late trees.
The road lies silver and quiet, leading just beyond the hill to
    the stars and the china yellow moon.
We said daffodils sprung on the mountain in the east after
    a chill dawn.
The hyacinth sky was there all the time, but dared not look at it.
Hills were everywhere.
Look, the mountains are ringed round and round with roads
    that look like white worms sleeping.
In Texas we said the plains are endless, silver on silver.
You can see where the sky begins, here, there, everywhere.
The sun is spread out like sheets of white metal over all the land.
The glare blinds you, and then the winds blow.
At night Orion stands on the town. Sirius staring there, just there
    above your head.
Aldebaran is a wicked eye, flaring from a dead giant.
Sleep, City, sleep.
The wagons rumble on the flatland roads.
Cattle cry to cattle and to the floating moon.
The frogs cry to the necessity for spring.

Photograph of Kathleen Tankersley young c. 1931–1933 by Jay Leyda,
The Museum of Modern Art, New York.

Postcard of the newly opened public school in Alpine, Texas, c. 1911. A news item in the Alpine Avalanche notes that the Tankersley family moved from Sanderson to Alpine on July 3, 1913 in order for Kathleen to attend the new school. Image via the Marfa Public Library.

Young's paternal grandparents. Left: Richard Franklin (R. F.) Tankersley (Feb. 19, 1828–Dec. 10, 1912). Above: Annie Eleanor Allen Tankersley (Mar. 16, 1928–Feb. 12, 1902). R. F. Tankersley is credited as one of the first cattlemen to settle in West Texas. The Tankersley Homestead outside of San Angelo, Texas, still stands today. Via ancestry.com

MOTHER ASKS DAUGHTER NOT TO LET DEATH STOP WEDDING

San Angelo, Texas, Feb. 2.—Wedding plans of Miss Kathleen Tankersley, daughter of a San Angelo ranchman, and Coulter Young of Hot Springs, Ark., were not disrupted Tuesday evening when Mrs. H. M. Tankersley, mother of the bride-to-be, died in a local sanitarium.

The wedding had been postponed on account of Mrs. Tankersley's illness, but it was her dying request that the ceremony immediately take place. Her wish was fulfilled two hours after her death. Frank B. Buchanan, Methodist pastor, who officiated at the wedding Tuesday, conducted Mrs. Tankersley's funeral late today. Mrs. Young was the only child.

Above: Kathleen's first husband, Henry Coulter Young, at the University of Texas, Austin, 1922.

Top left: A widely syndicated at the time of their marriage. This clipping is from *The Clifton Record*, Vol. 26, No. 47, Ed. 1 Friday, February 4, 1921, via The Portal to Texas History.

Bottom left: News item in the April 18, 1924 edition of the *Fort Worth Star-Telegram*, reporting the death of Young's father, H. M. "Mart" Tankersley in a wagon accident. Via newspapers.com.

Below: Kathleen's second husband, David Jerome Ellinger, in his West Point Yearbook, 1923.

SHEEP MAN KILLED IN TEAM RUNAWAY

SAN ANGELO, April 18.—Thrown beneath the wheels of a wagon when mules he was driving ran away, Henry Martin Tankersley, 59, San Angelo sheep man and member of a pioneer West Texas family, suffered injuries Wednesday that caused his death a few hours later at Rankin. The accident happened on the J. H. Massingill ranch. The body was buried at San Angelo yesterday.

Surviving are one daughter, Mrs. Kathleen Young of Kerrville; a brother, Fayette Tankersley of Mertzon, and three sisters, Mmes. Asa Frary, May Lewis and Elizabeth Emerick, all of San Angelo.

POETRY EXHIBIT NEWEST THING IN S. A.

There is something now in the literary world of San Antonio.

It is the poetry exhibit which opened at the Carnegie library Monday under the supervision of Kathleen Tankersley Young, a poet visiting in San Antonio.

The exhibit consists of a scrap book containing 500 poems chosen without discrimination from the pens of authors, known and unknown.

ORIGINAL POEMS.

Some of the poems are not even typewritten but remain in the handwriting of their authors. None has been published.

The book is only one of many which are being exhibited throughout the United States in a plan to assemble a thoroughly representative anthology of American verse. These scrap books have been assembled by Lou Ney and Ruth Willis Thompson of New York, who sponsor the movement.

Anyone may read the poems. All readers are asked to endorse their favorites. The endorsement is part of the method of selection for the anthology, which is to be entitled "The Antology of Little House Poetry."

TYPE VERSES.

Poems receiving as many as five endorsements will be uniformly typed after the exhibit and included in a second scrap book. Poetry lovers again will be asked to exercise their criticism when the second book is issued.

It is planned to include in a third book poems from the second scrapbook which receive as many as twenty-five endorsements. This process of elimination is to continue until finally 100 poems are chosen for the anthology. Authors of these 100 poems will be awarded prizes.

At left: Announcement for the arrival of the First National Poetry Exhibition in San Antonio in the *San Antonio Light*. Top right: Lew Ney hanging poems for the exhibition in New York, Graphic Arts Collection, Department of Rare Books and Special Collections, Princeton University Library. At bottom right: Lew Ney (left) with Ruth Widen (right) and her father (center), Scrapbook of the National Poetry Exhibition, New York Public Library.

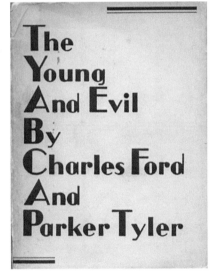

Clockwise from top left: Charles Henri Ford, photographed by Carl Van Vechten, c. 1933; the first issue of *Blues: A Magazine of New Rhythms*; the cover of the 1933 edition of Ford and Tyler's collaborative novel, *The Young and Evil*, which Ford dedicated to Kathleen; Parker Tyler, photographed by Carl Van Vechten, c. 1935. Photographs by Carl Van Vechten are reproduced with the generous permission of the The Carl Van Vechten Trust.

CHARLES HENRI FORD, Editor

B L U E S

A MAGAZINE OF NEW RHYTHMS

ROOMS 227-228 GILMER BLDG.
COLUMBUS, MISSISSIPPI

january 2 30

no, kathleen,

i wouldnt believe you hadnt written because
you hadnt thought of chrls when is the last
time i heard from kathleen id think i havent
,heard from kathleen in how many weeks
god honey dont eVeR do me that way again
never never never i recd your little
cmas crd and had one with your name on it
to send but i didnt know whaT address but
il send it now anyway LISTEN

im leaving here for new york on january
11, sailing from jacksonville on the 12th
arriving in nyc on the 15th im thrilled
pink about going plan to take three (3)
courses at the NeW School under Gorham
B. Munson, Harry Elmer Barnes and Fritz
Wittels. . il be there until summer
no doubt .. when when are you going back
tell me when god only that you were there
now pezzuZ. . .il probably work there
at something BLUES wont go on if i have to
keep it up for i cant you see in NY maybe
ads will maybe some publisher would like
to use it as an advertising medium and
print the thing for me why not ? if i do
get a chance to get it out il have to get
more material for i have accepted only about
enough for 24 pages!. . . lew ney will give
a BLUES night at his place with only Blues
poets on programe have you seen jan. NEW MASSES
Joseph Kalar has a poem in it which should
flatter you called Now That Show is Falling
it's unadulterated K T Y Kalar is a subscriber
to BLUES. cheyney makes a crack at BLUES in

Letter from Charles Henri Ford. After meeting Ford in San Antonio in the winter of 1928,
she would be instrumental in the founding and direction of Ford's *Blues: A Magazine of New
Rhythms*. Courtesy of Erik La Prade.

the jan nm too not to mention e. merril
root that bunch NAUSEATES me. The first
number of New World Monthly is out and i
like it. i have one poem in it also
parler tyler, lionel abel. book review
by munson. story by joseph mitchell.
i havent read it all. dial format, etc.

ALHAMBRA came. your six poems in it are the
best youve done since the six that were
in blues number one. i love them.

did you see my ($5.00) poem in BOOKS? please!

my poem in

not to mention ∧transition, jolas wrote
"Please give my apologies to Miss Young
for never acknowledging her letter. I
liked her story." he said my story was
scheduled for next number. also poems
by parker tyler. oh yes up stairs i have
a book sent you from paris by bob brown
il forward it tomorrow its a scream...

pagany ought ot be out by now im dying to
see it im dying to leave here il be dead
if you dont come to ny in the spring...

LISTEN il send you my address just as soon
as i get to ny and get one in the meantime
write me one (1) letter c/o parker tyler
hotel marlton, 3 west 8th street nyc
DO

    do love

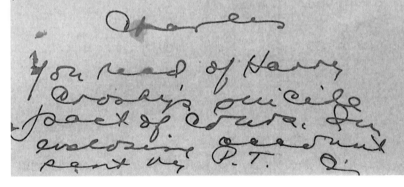

BEFORE DIVISION OF THE SUNS

TAKE SHEARS TO CUT A SECOND'S THREAD

THE MIND MUST TICK ECSTATIC ONCE

TO PROVE THAT IT IS DEAD.

Charled, My Dear-- I've only been able to read your last two
letters to night. Ive been desperately ill . . Still am. .
Have had a hurse with me night and day . . a still dark night
and a blue light burning somewhere and an overdose of morphine. .
then very cold . . and very tired . . and soft laughter like
sleep that ate away the sickly mind . . the rest struggling weakness
and ache of bones . . and ache of thoughts . . Now a clear light
burning that must thrust forth brilliant things lest I die of
them . .

This note a weary long thing of aching fingers and
tired eyes . . Here is a poem I happen to have nearby . .just
was rejected that the DIAL . . Four poems were just accepted
by OPPORTUNITY . . splendid poems of mine,too . .

I must stop . . Im exhausted . . surely Will be able to
write more soon . . I do love you Darling . . And I DO think
BLUES is wonderful . . We'll make it more.. Soon as I was able
to see I ask for BOOKS and saw the write-up . . It wasnt bad . .
Love, Chhrles, Dear,

Kathrin

Please write to me soon!

An undated letter to Charles Henri Ford (likely c. late 1929 or early 1930 by the reference to
poems accepted by *Opportunity*, published in April 1930), in which she mentions "an overdose
of morphine", via Beinecke Rare Book and Manuscript Library. The quatrain at the top of the
page is a partial quotation of Elinor Wylie's poem "Hospes Comesque Corporis".

Dear charles,

thanx for your letter and i
hdd intended answering long ago but many many
things have happened   was in the hospital here
in january and very ill from drinking absinth
had company too for many weeks

now i am writing and working and planning to
get away from here before long   yes i may go to
europe in may or june   or i may go back to NY
tell me when you are going to france or wherever
maybe we could go about the same time   but i
will go from here if i go, and i will go if i
can arrange the money side of it

here are some pictures   obviously

glad you liked THE SAD END   think O'Brien
must be using it for he asked me for a biographical
sketch for his book of best stories of the year and sent
it c/o Hound and Horn

had a letter from Bob Brown and he is in Cagnes
also Key Boyle Antheil, Gillespie, many others . . about forty in
all he said   and Morada is being published from there

have you seen Nativity and Front   Isaw the former Not
much good however   sorry that i let them have one of my best poems
i do not know about a story for blues as long as i can get money for
st ories i shall   poetry is what i must publish therefore i give it
away   you should see the letters about TEN POEMS: Valery Larbaud,
Herbert Read, Marianne Moore, Conrad Aiken, and Peter Quenell, all saying
good things   so after all you and tyler must have been wrong   i am so su
-e that i am NOT however# it doesnt matter   the book is good and is
even selling here and there

i hear from erskine caldwell now and then   also jay leyda   i
live for letters here   days are days with blue blue water and skies and
rain at night and the rapidly approaching rainy season   i have orchids
a collection of ten plants of them and one is budding   days slip off into
nothing

would be glad if you would send the magazines and books in Spanish
will you right away   give me something to do something to think about
I like Spanish but next to Frenth and German . . my french is improving
i often translate french poetry into english   but spanish poetry is too
silly most of it

write soon and i will write again   i like getting letters

Katht

3/21/31.

Letter to Charles Henri Ford dated March 21, 1931, including an apparent self-portrait, no longer intact (it is unclear who cut up the original photo), via Beinecke Rare Book and Manuscript Library.

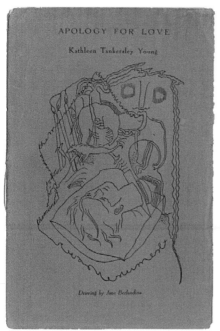

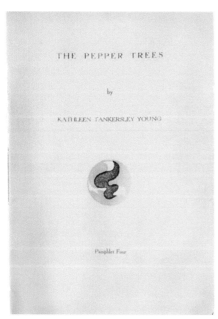

The four bound works published by Kathleen Tankersley Young, clockwise from top left: *Apology for Love*, Modern Editions Press (1933); *Ten Poems* (title page), Parnassus Press (1930); *The Dark Land*, The Dragon Press (1932); *The Pepper Trees*, Modern Editions Press (1932). Images of *Ten Poems* and *The Pepper Trees* courtesy Erik La Prade.

Selections of magazines featuring Young's work. Top row, from left: *The Hound & Horn*, Winter 1931; *The Echo*, October 1927; *Blues,* No. 8, Spring 1930. Middle row, from left: *The Houson Gargoyle,* April 14, 1929; *The Forge: A Midwestern Review*, Winter 1929; *Caravel* No. 5, March 1936 (edited by Charles Henri Ford). Bottom row, from left: *Transition* 16/17, June 1929; *Pagany* Vol. 1, No. 1, Winter 1930; *JAPM* May 27, 1929;

A flyer advertising the second series of The Modern Editions Press Pamphlet Series, which would include Kathleen's own *The Pepper Trees* and *Apology for Love* alongside work by Horace Gregory, Laurence Vail, Carl Rakosi, Raymond Ellsworth Larsson, Kay Boyle, and Bob Brown. Larsson, Rakosi, Vail, and Gregory pictured below. Images courtesy of Erik La Prade.

POISONED

Kathleen Tankersley Young, San Antonio poet and wife of Lieut. D. J. Ellinger, Duncan field, who drank poison in Torreon, Mexico, is shown above. She was found dead in her hotel room.

LAY POETESS' DEATH TO FEAR

A broken heart caused by the growing fear that she had lost her creative impulse apparently prompted Kathleen Tankersley Young to drink poison and die last Sunday night at her hotel in Torreon. Mexico, where ironically, she had gone to recapture her failing health.

Such was the belief expressed by acquaintances of the brilliant young San Antonio poet in Torreon, according to further details of the tragedy received here Thursday. She was the wife of Lieut. D. J. Ellinger, Duncan field, and was on the honor roll both at Harvard and Columbia.

The hotel keeper reported that four days prior to her death the young woman started to drink heavily and that she kept on drinking until the night of the tragedy.

Scattered about the floor of her room were fragments of poems and unfinished stories, indicating, acquaintances said, that she had tried repeatedly to satisfy the longing of her artistic heart to create something more. She was the author of several books of poems.

Nearest the bed which she made her bier was a fragmentary poem entitled "The Tourist Death," which acquaintances said possibly symbolized her own swift, tragic passing.

Friends in Torreon said that the young writer had complained of loneliness in Mexico and had expressed the fear she was losing her mental capacity and declared she wished to die in order to free her soul.

Funeral services will be held at the Wilbert-Hanavan chapel at 2 p. m. Saturday.

Two news items reporting on the death of Kathleen Tankersley Young, appearing on April 12 asnd 13, respectively, in the *San Antonio Light*.

Candid photos of Kathleen Tankersley Young, photographer(s) and date(s) unknown. Courtesy of Erik La Prade.

SELECTED
UNPUBLISHED
WORKS

Slowly into my strange straight eyes

"Three Poems for R.B.", *Two Preludes to a Marginal Darkness*

Slowly into my strange straight eyes
your curved smile
                    like mornings in april maybe
clearly blue mornings with fluttering wings of birds
falling into the street like rain
                              rises like a blue sound
everything now rocks to something else:
how when your small white hand has taken mine
and taught me all the wild sweetness of may
I shall be human again and stricken dumb:
I shall know under the slow smile (the touch)
mornings that are of the lost mornings:
                              april and sun:
                                   your curved smile.

For that your spirit has the quick brilliancy
of mornings in April

"Three Poems for R.B.", *Two Preludes to a Marginal Darkness*

For that your spirit has the quick brilliancy of mornings in April
so too your eyes bear blossoms of new light
and your pale lips the quiverings of white winds
say, your hand's touch is a huge
chilled white flower
through which swiftly music is blown into silence
o of your strange April self
                              a circle drawn bluely
across everything else in any manner remembered:
                                        only your hands.

Possessing now of you the white silence
of your touch

"Three Poems for R.B.", *Two Preludes to a Marginal Darkness*

Possessing now of you the white silence of your touch
your fast remembered smile climbs the blue circle of my mind:
you are a flower: and April will break you:
I am a stone: and a stone's darkness:
under the slow silence of your touch
the April suddenness of all your singing self
belies such darkness:
               of the dark: myself:
only of stones and the knowledge of darkness:
                        these: myself:
and the slow newly vibrant music wavering on your little mouth:
and your remembered smile lying sweetly on my dead black dream.

The hours fall off like little leaves

The hours fall off like little leaves
Through an autumn afternoon,
Float downward, motionless and dead:
The days fall off,
A thousand of them
Fall, one by one, without a sound:
After the falling a thin moon slips
To a gold hill, and is consumed later by white waters
It is taken by lovers for an image,
And remembered as a sign long after,
Long after this water-devoured moon is dead:
Here is no winter with the tight icebuds,
But only days, suns, moons, that have a dropping off
Noticeable in letters received and answered,
In months glanced from the calendar:
The barrenness is slow, but certain, fixed.

And now

And now
doors and walls, holding the late silence,
the sound of huddled waters
waiting moonfall:
                    QUICK   quick

                                your kiss

AFTERNOON SNOW

Two Preludes to a Marginal Darkness

Perfume thickens on the air,
                    Perfume
Of many women walking through the gloom,
And in the park, the yellow trees grow
Deep in the winter wind, with blowing snow.

Now in the dark afternoon, perfume
Will color and reshape the gloom.
A gull blows inland.
                    And I shall sleep.
Wind is a part of what I keep.
Gulls are a part of what I know.
And women, and perfume, and whirling snow.

POEM

Two Preludes to a Marginal Darkness

The round and silver lamp, taking this room
has twisted music from the crystals
on her arm; has wrung from the gloom
a third dimension of the circle walls:

We sit bent threewise,
and her hands now larger than her head
stretch forward to her eyes
now motionless and dead.

POEM

Two Preludes to a Marginal Darkness

What now but the lone black swan
where petals drift upon these solemn waters,
slow under the pale sungrapes swinging downward
where no reality of reflection lives:
the marked sun a thin silk upon these cool waters,
and the mood of dream floats like a dark sleep
flowing onward to the lips of rivers:
                     still knowing nothing,
marking nothing, where does the self begin?
black image in a blackened water,
                     where does the mirror end?
                            what now
but the lone black swan,
          slow to a mirrorself long known,
begings the ancient sleep and dream.

These cannot be broken

Two Preludes to a Marginal Darkness

These cannot be broken:
The lands, the rocks, the tulips, in springshine,
And your inscrutable heart still ticking:
And that in myself there is no beginning,
Certainly no ending:
                    The wind comes up
And the sound of rain like weeping,
Waters too come up from islands:
From what islands I have asked,
And have been answered:
Islands to walk upon, to know,
To feel the sound of,
Islands I shall later know,
And lands with names
That we have spoken.
Ulysses not forgotten,
Not the names of islands,
Not Penelope waiting,
                    Not your hands.

We began at morning and it was this way

Two Preludes to a Marginal Darkness

We began at morning and it was this way
We passed through the trees and had no feeling
the sunshine was left behind
We met a thin girl
A good figure to meet on the roadway at morning
With roses on one side flowering under thick glasses
And the left bank burned black by fires
And beyond the sunshine upward a little
Voices together among the trees on the hilltop
And later and later our footsteps clacking separately down
    the road beyond the hill

In November the cold waterbirds

City Without Images

In November the cold waterbirds
Float in their circles under a cooling sky,
With no body mirrored under,
With no sun over:
Slower to their movement,
Swifter to their crying,
They are floated, they are circled,
Their heads hang downward like cold lead:
When winter comes, steel to the ponds,
The waterbirds walk on the cold stones,
On the twigs, on the snow, marking their ways,
Walking in a frozen dream:
They are awake: they are dead:
They are as all fast walkers
Having but a soundless movement
Moving in a sleep,
Heavy, golden.

POEM

Two Preludes to a Marginal Darkness

My worlds have whirled in polished cups and spoons,
And in the black waters rotting a thousand moons:
My surface worlds have mirrored a thin distorted hand,
A tragic mouth, a walking movement in a yellow land,
A leaf falling downward, the rounded measurement
Of circle pools where images are bent:
But these worlds have vanished before I measured out
The thinness or the thickness of the burning doubt.

VENICE IN THE YEAR OF THIS, MY FLOWERING

Two Preludes to a Marginal Darkness

Venice
in the year of this,
my flowering,
          staring at trees coldly in water,
and my own reflected head,
                    Venice (remembered)
                                   in the year of this
my mouth leaning to your mouth,
leaning to a first awakening,
                    Venice, now, is dead.

along the streets where now
the paling leaves
are frozen closer to the older bough,
i go to renounce the flowering of trees,
and hear forever like the sound of wind, our kiss
hovering where only darkness is.

SLEEPING DEATH

City Without Images

Make clear the sharpened edges of our two selves
Who pressed our hands together, and our mouths
As through a sheet of glass which rendered up the image
Without the actual touch, the voice without the words:
We heard the tulips crossing their roots under the snow
We remembered the lone swan in the cold lakes forgotten:
But nothing has happened,
Although the mind traverses all these things freely:
My hand lies in the broken light
Upon a worn book, the same.

if

if

    i to myself upon this hour do now declare the shell is dead
and never to be trumpeted in roses in another dawn musics
waver on a soul that is to be forever lost where wander winds
calky with birds and heavy with leaffall the self that wavers
whispers now the thirtieth declaration of the end

POEM

City Without Images

For you have come upon my heart
As frost comes to the foot-hills in September,
Though the leaves tremble, and the rocks chill
I know this promises a long death, a suddenness
Of snow in the frail night time,
A beating on winds upon black rocks,
And a nothingness:
But think, there shall be other lovers, who in the Spring
Return the flowers to the melting lakes,
And birds to the trees that shower music:
But when the winters return,
Always it is you who will bereave me
In a hundred winters, in a hundred winds,
In a hundred rocks, a hundred trees,
And the sudden acknowledgment of these.

POEM

Two Preludes to a Marginal Darkness

I go today to find the hill of leaves deserted
And beneath the hill, the same swans whirling,
As if they knew my sorrow to be
The shadow standing between the hill and water:
You had walked here on the snow
Lightly for in fear of crushing crocus leaves:
You sensed the crisp white fragile violets
Through the crystal ice on every hill:
The frozen pond became a mirror for your dream,
Where you saw the Spring breaking as through a frosted glass.
Now you have gone from this hill,
The swan does not remember, nor the wind,
And the late ice that you walked upon had melted to
    the silver lake:
To what land have you gone?
What Spring is there? The late hot flowers,
Or the early aloofness of blossoms out of snow banks?
What motion stirs this April in your mind?

VOYAGE OF THE HEART

City Without Images

From winter waters I have gone
Hungering no more,
But moving with precision toward a southern sea,
Having found nothing to stir the mind grown quiet,
Come so sudden from a brilliant heaven:
Leaves and silver clouds are whirled
Across the year, and the snow comes to the far hills,
Rabbits run, and the ponds freeze:
But sailing here toward palms
Forever swept by winds from warming waters,
I have set my body to the sea,
Relinquishing the lands, the white buildings,
For a tropic sleep:
I have forgotten streets turning with wind,
The breaking of glass in the courtyards,
The cut flowers for sale on the sidewalks,
I have forgotten little rooms warm and dark
Coming from a thick rainfall:
I go to the tropic islands,
I, wasted and grown thin, no longer flowering,
Too late I wander to the breadfruit trees,
To the whitened beaches, to the greening days:
Too late the voyage of the heart,
The heart turned barren,
And the winter come forever to the blinded mind:
Too late the voyage of the heart.

Colors of blue at evening,
Trees standing in sun on tropic isles,
Great birds waking and crying on the long sands:
It is come too late:
Still the body, lucid and pliable,
The feeble senses excited,
Sits in the darkness on the cold deck chairs,
The eyes stare out, the body wears white, or golden,
And sleeps at intervals between the waking,
And still walks through the silver winds
Come fresh from the lateral direction:
The mouth has words given to many faces,
The hands that touch and move, and touch with other hands:
But this come too late.

The voyage of the heart continues:
It is cold at night, and I stare for hours at the rocking stars:
And thinking that the end occurs before the beginning:
The voyage continues, through winter waters
Drifting slowly southward;
There are times I remember your voice,
And remember what it awakens in my brain:
I hold the thought of this at night, while sleeping,
To my barren heart, my dying mind:
Why have we never talked of an ending.
In your voice there is only a beginning,
And a beginning, a seventh beginning:
As your voice carries this music
In a barren land, to a dying brain.

POEM FOR AUTUMN

Two Preludes to a Marginal Darkness

leaves,
scattered by water,
will lie
knowing no further image
and the water drink them down by sun's edge,
or under moon, made little by the treeless dark.
or, if from the shell of wind,
a single leaf is drawn by air,
the water, stirring, sweep all gold
back to the roots, dead in the sun,
or under the moon,
the late scattering dark leaves.

(for such is the knowledge)

(for such is the knowledge)
and little boys walk on roses
carrying morning,
but i, walking on frostkill
have seen the day shot like a black bullet
into this self:
little boys whistle, walking on yellow roses,
where the frostkill and the silence
blows over, and the day is shot
like a leaden bullet
into a self leaning among the dead branches
of frostleaf, listening faroff
little boys whistling gaily a thousandth yellow morning:
(these are not mind)
(for such is the knowledge)
(for such IS) and little boys walk
on roses, strangled by the sunlight of the day.

THERE ARE NO DARKER THINGS THAN THESE

City Without Images

There are no darker things than these:
Leaf and shadow under autumn rain,
Mornings without sun, and barren trees
That turn and blow and freeze again.

There are no stranger things that one
May sense, that one may come upon:
Darkness whirling back of the sun,
A kinship to a cold black stone.

The day drowns, and the grey rains mark
The buildings, change their color and their shape:
And rain keeps falling through the imaged dark
Turning the gold leaf, chilling the ripe grape.

There are no darker images than
These I circle with my mind.
No world could be darker. No man
Has ever gone more starkly blind.

FRAGMENT

Two Preludes to a Marginal Darkness

fifth dimension to my dark
i hear them singing and that song
is washed by wind:
i feel outward with my hands to know your hand
and do not understand
how curiously they grow so cool, how marvelously cool,
and take the winter wholly to my heart.

FRAGMENT

Two Preludes to a Marginal Darkness

As one who blinded had forgot the sun
I stand knowing the dark
to be forever settled in myself
and remembering the hot noons that poured
intense and sickening silence in the streets
I then renounce the mornings, and the moon

The birds from thin trees, dead

City Without Images

The birds from thin trees, dead
In their flower, suspend music slowly,
Music like a slender thread,
Until the morning bursts its mirror shell, and is to be
Split threewise
To your goldeneyes:
                    But nothing has ended when the birds
From trees, globular in sun, suspend a net of words,
Though you cannot know, nor sense, nor guess
A world hung sunwise, perpendicular, motionless.

Beloved, we two have been discovered

Beloved, we two have been discovered
As have the yellow leaves,
Or the sunlight laughing among light branches,
Or the hills holding their mirror ponds to the sky:
Our story is the old flight of lovers,
Yours and mine:
It is not different: it is not timeless:
We are not yet voiceless: we will remain;
Remain as long as the yellow violets,
The crying birds,
We will remain to dance after the music has been forgotten,
But with other lovers,
Other dreams.

And if the slow decaying root

Two Preludes to a Marginal Darkness

And if the slow decaying root
Under the spell of rain and mud
Be somewhat confused with thought of fruit
Though a dead root yields no food,

Under the cold stones where water smoothes
The last sweet folds of dust between
The dreams of roots, dark will use
The ultimate thought of growing green:

Now images are crushed beneath a stone:
The print of roots are slow and dead:
Where roses sprange, a brittle bone
Is fed.

And now in the ground the stark
Roots crumble and waver:
And here now in the stony dark
Only the sound grows of seeping water.

the trees remind us

Two Preludes to a Marginal Darkness

the trees remind us
Diana gone from her hill
our heads gone from the teacups
the moon consuming the mountains
but of our hands no more the syllables of fingers
making known another body, and another breath:

no more the winter in her silver
in her sleeping, tapping at the frosted pane,
our heads leaning together
seeking out the streets, the figures,
and the voices in the snow.

no more the heron on december tropic waters
blowin in the wind from swamp to beach
and crying their thin notes of contentment,
our minds pressed together,
awaiting another sort of flowering,
and a northern spring.

no more my hand, come up from the coffin
leaning downward toward plucked roses,
and the people staring, and the music still forever,
but always forever in my head the whirr
that continues forever in all universes
faster faster, and the remembrance of beauty
before the knowledge of nothingness
before the dark.

This hard mirror is a record

City Without Images

This hard mirror is a record:
Your eyes and hair, your lips and gestures
Move in this surface: and I stand
Touching your shoulder, murmuring: Spring:
The sun beyond the window shouts yellow.
We are consumed.
Soon we will lie down to sleep
Breathing a coolness,
Trying not to think:
We are dead, and have but a floating memory:
It were better that this were dead, too,
And that we were led through all the streets
Begging coins from cool and perfumed hands,
Feeling the wind.
This hard mirror is a record, we are turned toward it,
But cannot see,
And outward everywhere, the sun.

LILY

City Without Images

This lily now will never bloom:
The confused traces of perfume
Will be eaten by the frailest leaves
Thrusting up the slightest images:

And leaf on leaf the silver green
Will grow higher, but between
The unborn buds, the light will feed
The lily's least urgent need.

Strange that we sleep and then awaken

City Without Images

Strange that we sleep and then awaken
And remember nothing
We see figures on the white page
And the words are August and the red first
And we learn that ships are lifted from old waters
And that a stronger light is used, just having been invented
And that in an old house a young girl died
Having first scrawled on a paper;
And seeing the date, we turn,
We sleep through August and the wind begins
To pull at the strange houses
And we reconstruct these houses and these streets
Within our dreams, and we have moods without
Any movement, and they do not flow easily about us
We sleep with the curtains drawn,
And sort out the self that will awaken
And wear a certain dress and drink a cup of tea;
Sunshine rains into the street
When we draw aside the curtains,
And out we go beyond this street,
Beyond, and these people swallow us
What are they saying
They are talking of yesterday
I turn my pale hand: the people look:
In it I see blood and suddenly I see the print
Of your nail and suddenly you
You, but what are they saying

They are talking of yesterday
Blue smoke and farewell
Every morning the street is filled with goodbyes,
And I come to the end of this sleeping;
After a while I say goodbye to Sleeping Margaret
And the dark:
I go beyond these streets, beyond these houses
And the people swallow me
And I know nothing;
It is August however the papers tell me
And that a hundred people have died and been buried;
Later beyond these streets I will find some gesture
That will return me, by which I can remember yesterday:
And then we shall be, and dance through all the streets
Just after twilights, the roofs glistening
With light, with the great light just invented:
And no more the darkness,
And no more the dark.

POEM

Two Preludes to a Marginal Darkness

Along the streets where now
The paling leaves
Are frozen closer to the bough,
I go to renounce the flowering of all trees,
And hear forever like the sound of wind, our kiss
Hovering where only darkness is.

Leave me

City Without Images

Leave me   leave me
The room closes in upon me with wind
The streets become voiceless
We shall live among the snows
And speak to each other in a foreign tongue
Do so, for you will continue
From those sleeping beyond the windows
I have done:
In the cold lakes that are not of my country
I will lie and let the midnight carry me far
My country was the country of sudden flowers
And heat and the fear of rebels
I do not ever care to remember
We have toiled in the night and taken nothing.

I shall be hungry when I think of you

Letter to Charles Henri Ford, May 8, 1928

I shall be hungry when I think of you
I shall be fed
By other hands
Though this will not satisfy till I am dead...

A BIOGRAPHICAL TIMELINE

August 15, 1902: Kathleen Tankerlsey is born to H. M. "Mart" Tankersley and Mary Tankersley née Hudspeth, in rural west Texas, likely in Sonora, the closest town with a hospital to the family's ranch near the Dry Devil's River, where Mart Tankersley bought land for a sheep ranch in 1898.

July 3, 1913: Tankersley family moves to Alpine, Texas for Kathleen to attend the newly opened Alpine School

February 8, 1918: According to the *Alpine Avalanche*, Kathleen is part of the Sophomore Literary Society at San Angelo High School

February 1, 1921: On the same day that her mother passes away, Kathleen marries Henry Coulter Young of Hot Springs, Arkansas. A widely syndicated news item reports that it was Kathleen's mother's dying wish for her daughter's marriage to go on as planned

October 1921: Henry Young is listed as being a senior at the University of Texas at Austin and a clarinetist in the famous Longhorn Band

1923–1925: Young was listed as a member of the Poetry Society of Texas, registered under her birth name. She and Henry Young buy land in San Angelo, Texas, near Fort Concho At some point in this period, she and her husband move to Denver, Colorado

April 16, 1924: H. M. Tankersley dies after falling in front of a loaded wagon while in Rankin, Texas

February 10, 1925: Henry Young dies of tuberculosis at home in Malvern, Arkansas, not far from Hot Springs, where he was born.

June 13, 1926: The first known poem by Kathleen Tankersley Young, "To a Friend", appears in the *Houston Post-Dispatch*. Her address is listed as being in San Antonio, Texas

January 11, 1927: Moves to Austin, Texas, as noted in the *Austin American*

1927: Joins *The Echo*, a literary magazine based in Denver and published by David Raffelock, as an editor. The publication of her poem "Tribute" in *The Gypsy* indicates her place of residence as Denver

February 28, 1928: Meets the poet Charles Henri Ford, age 20 and a freshman at St. Mary's College, at the Carnegie Library in San Antonio while she is exhibiting a scrapbook of poems from the First National Poetry Exhibition provided to her for that purpose by the New York City printer Lew Ney (Luther Widen). Ney wrote to her on February 15, suggesting she drop Ford a line. Ford and Young begin an intense professional and personal relationship

1928: Rejoins the Poetry Society of Texas for the year, this time registering as Kathleen Tankersley Young. She agrees to serve as associate editor for Ford's new magazine, *Blues: A Magazine of New Rhythms*

On April 21, she writes to Ford of a "hemmorhage from the stomach" and a dire warning from doctors to rest. She reports to Ford that she has an unspecified operation scheduled at the Medical Arts Hospital in San Antonio for June 27. In a July letter to Lew Ney and Ruth Widen, she mentions taking morphine to relieve pain

1929: Indicates in letters that she is suffering from both health issues (an "illness from which I can't seem to recover", mentioned in a January 16 letter for Ford) and depression, writing to Ford on March 4 that "I have been on the verge of suicide the last few days."

July 10, 1929: Married Air Force Lieutenant David Jerome (D.J.) Ellinger in a civil ceremony in Nuevo Laredo, Mexico. She appears to have returned to New York shortly thereafter, writing to Charles Henri Ford on August 14 that she was going to live alone, downtown

November 1, 1929: Submits the manuscript *Two Preludes to a Marginal Darkness* to the Yale Series of Younger Poets. In her cover letter, she gives her date of birth as April 15, 1903, and her birthplace as Cincinnati, Ohio

November 4, 1929: Meets Angel Flores in New York, at the time, editor of *Alhambra*. A series of letters from Flores to Young indicates an affair between the two

November 22, 1929–May 9, 1930: Visits Panama, where Ellinger is stationed. Traveling by boat, she lists her date of birth as August 15, 1905 and place of birth as New York City on the passenger manifest

1930: *Ten Poems* is published by Parnassus Press, though Kathleen would pay for the publication herself, owing installments to Lew Ney and Ruth Widen

1930-1931: Mentions a morphine overdose in an undated letter to Charles Henri Ford

Late 1931: Begins the Modern Editions Press pamphlet series, with Eric Naul, a figure who left an even scarcer historical record than Young, and who may, we believe, have never existed

1932: The Modern Editions Press publishes *The Pepper Trees*, a collection of three stories. *The Dark Land: Poems* is published by Angel Flores's Dragon Press

1933: A standalone pamphlet of "Apology for Love", which first appeared in *The Dark Land*, is published by Modern Editions Press

April 9, 1933: Dies in a hotel room in Torreón, Mexico at 10:30pm. A report filed by J. Frank Points, the American Vice Consul in Mexico, states that she had been in a coma-like state from morphine, other opiates, and alcoholic drinks and was unable to talk. The same account noticed that she had been "running around Saltillo and Torreón for the past three to four weeks with a man by the name of Abdon Hernandez Navarro". Her official cause of death is listed as "taking lysol poisoning". It was ruled a suicide

ACKNOWLEDGMENTS

This book could not have come together without the preservation of libraries public and private, and we are forever grateful for that. The following institutions are owed a great debt of gratitude for taking our calls and emails: New York Public Library; Houston Public Library; Cleveland Public Library; Cincinnati Public Library; Seattle Public Library; Case Western University Library; the Ohio Historical Society; the Poetry Society of Texas; the Washington State University Library; Vanderbilt University Special Collections; the Stuart A. Rose Manuscript, Archives, and Rare Book Library at Emory University; Case Western Reserve University Archives; Beinecke Rare Book Library; Yale University Library; New Mexico State University Library; San Angelo State University Library; Dallas Public Library; Denver Public Library; Princeton University Library; and the Internet Archive.

Erik La Prade: I particularly want to thank Charles Henri Ford for first introducing me to Kathleen Tankersley Young's work. Also, Brice Brown and Don Joint for inviting me to write an article on Young and publishing it in their magazine, *TETHER* #3, 2017. Thanks also to Abbey Kupersmith and Robert Ghiradella, for their critical input as readers of Young's work.

Joshua Rothes: I would like to extend special thanks to my co-editor, Erik La Prade, for keeping the memory of Kathleen Tankersley Young alive and preserving so many of the materials that made this book possible. And of course, to the individuals who assisted us in one way or another: Mike and Karen Tankersley, Jacob Siefring, Christina Tudor-Sideri, Hind Fiddah, Craig Saper, and Eric White.

THE EMPYREAN SERIES

about
The Empyrean Series is an imprint of
Sublunary Editions, dedicated to producing
new editions of overlooked works from the
history of world literature.

editors
Jacob Siefring, Joshua Rothes

design
Joshua Rothes

web
sublunaryeditions.com/empyrean

etc
Empyrean Series titles are printed on acid-
free, post-consumer paper.

THE EMPYREAN CATALOGUE